CONTENTS.

CHAPTER XIV.

1727—1760.

BOOK THE SECOND.

OF MYSELF.

CHAPTER I.

CHAPTER II.

CHAPTER III.

CHAPTER IV.

CHAPTER V.

1763—1778.

CHAPTER VI.

1778.

CHAPTER VII.

1782.

CHAPTER VIII.

CHAPTER IX.

1782—1795.

CHAPTER X.

CHAPTER XI.

1793—1796.

CHAPTER XII.

1798—1800.

MEMOIRS

OF

CAPTAIN ROCK.

———◆———

BOOK THE FIRST.

———

OF MY ANCESTORS.

———

Genus antiquum terræ.
(VIRGIL.)

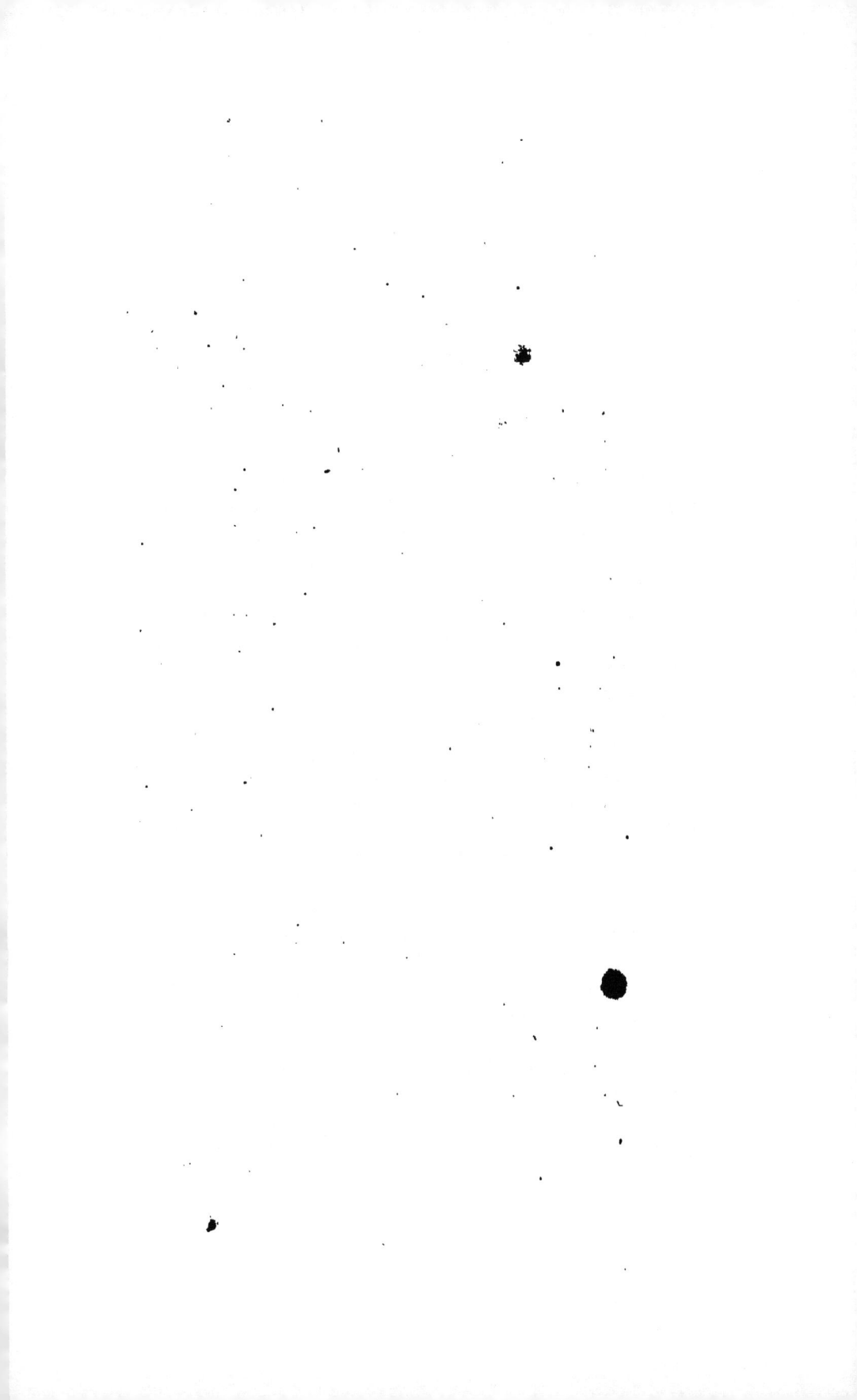

PREFACE

BY THE EDITOR.

In introducing to the Reader the following account of Captain Rock, it may be as well that I should also give him some account of myself, and of the manner in which the Manuscript of the Captain came into my possession.

I little thought, at one time of my life, that I ever should be induced to visit Ireland. Often, indeed, had I declared— so great was my horror of that country—that " I would just as soon trust my person among those savages of the Andamans, who eat up all new-comers, as among the best bred gentlemen of Kerry and Tipperary." The circumstances that at length led me to muster up courage enough for the undertaking, were as follow :—

In the small town of ——— where I reside, in the West of England, some pious persons succeeded, the year before last, in establishing a Society on the model of the Home Missionary in London ;—with this difference, that the labours of the latter are principally confined to England, while ours were chiefly, if not exclusively, directed to the conversion and illumination of the poor benighted Irish.

The Ladies of our Town, in particular, were so impressed with the urgency of raising that unfortunate race from darkness, that every moment of delay in sending Missionaries among them, appeared, as it were, an age lost to the good cause. " What could be more imperative," they asked, " than the claims of those destitute souls upon us ?—If the County of Worcester, which has hitherto been accounted the Garden of England, is now (as the Report of the Home

Missionary assures us) become, for want of preachers, 'a
waste and a howling wilderness,' [1] what must the mountains
of Macgillicuddy be?"

In this temper of our little community, it was my lot to
be singled out—as knowing more of Catholic countries than
the rest, from having passed six weeks of the preceding
summer at Boulogne—to undertake the honourable, but
appalling task of Missionary to the South of Ireland.

To hint any thing of my personal fears to the Ladies (all
Christians as they were), was more than I had the courage
to venture. As a brave man once said, to excuse himself
for not refusing some coxcomb's challenge, "I might safely
trust to the judgment of my sex, but how should I appear
at night before the maids of honour?"

I, accordingly, prepared myself as speedily as I could for
the undertaking; and read every book relating to Ireland
that was at all likely to furnish me with correct notions on
the subject. For instance, in every thing relating to political
economy and statistics, I consulted Sir John Carr—for accurate details of the rebellion of 1798, Sir Richard Musgrave—and for statesman-like views of the Catholic Question,
the speeches of Mr. Peel.

I was also provided by our Society with a large assortment
of Religious Tracts, written expressly for the edification of
the Irish peasantry; particularly, a whole edition of a little
work by Miss —— of our Town, to the effect of which upon
the Whiteboys we all looked forward very sanguinely.

With the details of my journey to Dublin I shall not
trouble the reader, nor with any account of the curiosities
which I witnessed during my short stay in that city. I visited, of course, the Parliament House, which is a melancholy
emblem of departed greatness. In the House of Lords, the
only relic of its former pomp is a fragment of an old chan-

---

[1] "The Rev. Timothy East, of Birmingham, states, in a published
Sermon, which we earnestly recommend to the attention of the public,
that the County of Worcester has been termed the Garden of England;
but; in a moral light, it may be regarded as *a waste, a howling wilderness.*"

delier, which they show mournfully to strangers, as " the last remaining *branch* of the Aristocracy"—and the part of this structure which *was* the House of Commons, is, since the Union, by a natural transition, converted into a *Cash* office.

Having received all proper instructions from the manager of the Religious Tract Establishment in Sackville Street (to whom our fellow-labourers of the London Tavern had consigned me), I left Dublin in the Limerick Coach, on the 16th of July, 1823, in company with a gentleman who wore green spectacles and a flaxen wig, and who was, in many other respects, a very extraordinary personage.

As he was one of those people, who prefer monologue to dialogue, he talked through the whole journey, and I listened to him with exemplary patience.

The first place of any note, on our way, was Náas—near which there is the ruin of a magnificent house, begun, but never finished, by Lord Strafford, when Lord Lieutenant of Ireland. In pointing it out to me, my friend in the green spectacles said :—" It is melancholy to think, that while in almost all other countries, we find historical names of heroes and benefactors, familiarly on the lips of the common people, and handed down with blessings from generation to generation, in Ireland, the only remarkable names of the last six hundred years, that have survived in the popular traditions of the country, are become words of ill omen, and are remembered only to be cursed. Among these favourites of hate, the haughty nobleman who built that mansion, is to this day, with a tenacity that does honour even to hate, recorded ; and, under the name of Black Tom, still haunts the imagination of the peasant, as one of those dark and evil beings who tormented the land in former days, and with whom, in the bitterness of his heart, he compares its more modern tormentors. The Babylonians, we are told by Herodotus, buried their dead in honey—but it is in the very gall of the heart that the memory of Ireland's rulers is embalmed."

From his use of metaphors, and abuse of the Government, I should have concluded that my companion was a genuine Irishman—even if the richness of his brogue had not established his claim to that distinction.

In passing by the town of Kildare he directed my attention to the still existing traces of that ruin and havoc which were produced by the events of the year 1798—" one of those ferocious rebellions (as he expressed himself) whose frequent recurrence has rendered Ireland, even in her calmest moments, like those fair cities on the side of Vesuvius, but a tenant at will to the volcano on which she is placed!

" Is not this singular?" he added, "is not this melancholy? That, while the progress of time produces a change in all other nations, the destiny of Ireland remains still the same— that here we still find her, at the end of so many centuries, struggling, like Ixion, on her wheel of torture—never advancing, always suffering—her whole existence one monotonous round of agony! While a principle of compensation is observable throughout the fortunes of all the rest of mankind, and they, who enjoy liberty, must pay for it by struggles, and they, who have sunk into slavery, have, at least, the consolation of tranquillity—in *this* unhappy country it is only the *evil* of each system that is perpetuated —eternal struggles, without one glimpse of freedom, and an unrelaxing pressure of power, without one moment of consolidation or repose!"

At Roscrea, about half-way between Dublin and Limerick, I parted with this gentleman—having, in the course of conversation, communicated to him the object of my journey to the South, at which I observed he smiled rather significantly.

From Roscrea I turned off the main road, to pay a visit to an old friend, the Rev. Mr. ——, whom I found comfortably situated in his new living, with the sole drawback, it is true, of being obliged to barricade his house of an evening, and having little embrasures in his hall-door to fire through at unwelcome visitors.

In the neighbourhood of my friend's house there are the ruins of a celebrated abbey, which stand, picturesquely enough, on the banks of the river, and are much resorted to by romantic travellers. A wish had, more than once, occurred to me to see the effect of these ruins by moonlight; but the alarming indications of the gun-holes in the hall-door had prevented me from entertaining any serious thoughts of such an enterprize.

On the third evening of my stay, however, the influence of the genial "mountain dew,"[1] which my Reverend host rather bountifully dispensed, so far prevailed over my fears and my prudence, that I sallied forth, alone, to visit these ruins.

Of my walk I have no very clear recollection. I only remember that from behind the venerable walls, as I approached them, a confused murmur arose, which startled me for a moment—but all again was silent, and I cautiously proceeded. Just then, a dark cloud happened to flit over the moon, which, added to the effects of the "mountain dew," prevented me from seeing the objects before me very distinctly. I reached, however, in safety the great portal of the abbey, and passing through it to the bank which overhangs the river, found myself all at once, to my astonishment and horror (the moon at that moment breaking out of a cloud), in the midst of some hundreds of awful-looking persons—all arrayed in white shirts, and ranged in silent order on each side to receive me!

This sight sobered me completely—I was ready to sink with terror—when a voice, which, I could observe, proceeded from a tall man with a plume of white feathers in his hat,[2] said, sternly, "Pass on," and I, of course, promptly obeyed. Though there was something in the voice, that

---

[1] Whiskey, "that has never seen the face of a gauger."
[2] Hickey, a *Pseudo* Captain Rock, who was hanged last summer at Cork, appears to have generally worn feathers in his nightly expeditions.

seemed rather familiar to my ears, it was not without exceeding horror that I perceived the figure that spoke advance out of the ranks and slowly follow me.

We had not gone many steps, when I politely motioned to him to take precedence—not feeling quite comfortable with such a goblin after me. He, accordingly, went before, and having conducted me to a spot, at some distance from the band, where we could not be observed by them, turned hastily round, and took me, with much cordiality, by the hand.

I now perceived—what the reader must have anticipated —that this personage was no other than the disguised gentleman in green spectacles; nor was it long before I learned, from his own lips, that I then actually stood in the presence of the great CAPTAIN ROCK.

What passed between the Captain and me at that interview, I do not feel myself, as yet, at liberty to reveal. I can only state that it was in the course of that short meeting, he presented me with the Manuscript which I have now the honour of submitting to the Public—requesting of me, as a favour, that I would read it attentively over, before I threw away any further labour or thought upon the mission which I had undertaken.

I lost no time, as may easily be supposed, in complying with the Captain's wish. That very night, before I slept, I carefully perused the whole of his Manuscript; and so strong was the impression it left upon my mind, that it is the Rulers, not the People of Ireland, who require to be instructed and converted, that I ordered horses early next morning— returned with all possible dispatch to my constituents—called instantly a full meeting of the Ladies of the Society, and proposed that a new mission should forthwith be instituted, for the express purpose of enlightening certain Dignitaries both of Church and State, who are, in every thing that relates to Ireland, involved in the most destitute darkness.

The ladies listened to my proposal with apparent interest, but no steps have, as yet, been taken on the subject—and the only result of my communication to them has been a Romance by Miss ———, on the story of Captain Rock, which is, at present, I understand, in the printer's hands, and which I shall not be surprised to find much more extensively read than the Captain's own authentic Memoirs.

With respect to the style of the following pages, though frequently rambling and ill-constructed, it will, I have no doubt, surprise the reader, as being much more civilized and correct than could be expected from a hero like the Captain. The classical quotations will also excite some surprise—but this kind of learning was once very common among persons of his rank in Ireland; and Smith, in his History of Kerry, tells us, "that classical reading extends itself, even to a fault, among the lower orders of Ireland—many of whom have a greater knowledge in this way, than some of the better sort in other places."

S. E.

March 31, 1824.

MEMOIRS

OF

CAPTAIN ROCK.

BOOK THE FIRST.

CHAPTER I.

A. M. 1.—A. D. 1172.

Antiquity of the Rocks.—Reign of Ollam Fodlah, Dubhlachtha, Flabhertach, etc.—Moran's Collar.—Chief-Justice Bushe.—Beautiful young
Lady.—Revolution among the Letters of the Irish Alphabet.—Name
of Rock, whence derived.—The Irish proved to be Jews.—Moral Character of the Rocks.

THE ROCKS are a family of great antiquity in Ireland; as old,
at least, as the "ancient family of the Wrongheads" in England.

That we had made some noise, even before the memorable period, when Pope Adrian made a present of Ireland to Henry II.,
there is every reason to believe; but under such wise monarchs
as Ollam Fodlah, Dubhlachtha, Flabhertach, Brian Boromhe, etc.,
whose laws, as Mr. O'Halloran assures us, were models of perfection, it was difficult even for the activity of the ROCKS to distinguish
itself. Accordingly, for the first 1100 years of the Christian era, we
hear but little or nothing of the achievements of the family.

There is, indeed, one remarkable circumstance, connected with
the administration of justice in those times, which may account
for the tranquillity and good order which, we are told, prevailed.
The chief judge, on all solemn and interesting occasions, had a
kind of collar placed round his neck [1], which possessed the wonderful power of contracting or relaxing, according to the impartiality of the sentence pronounced by him, and which pinched
most inconveniently when an unjust decision was uttered. The use
of this collar has been since discontinued, on account of the risk of

---

[1] Called, from the name of one of their most just judges, "Moran's collar."
Even to this day (says O'Halloran), in litigations between people, *by the judgment of Moran's collar* is a most solemn appeal.

strangulation to which it exposed many honourable judges, and
the collar itself was supposed to be lost; but, to the inexpressible
joy of all lovers of Irish curiosities, it was again discovered a short
time since, and is at present, I understand, worn on all occasions
by the chief-justice of Ireland, with the greatest possible ease and
comfort to himself.

We may imagine how dull my ancestors must have found those
times, when a beautiful young lady (as Dr. Warmer tells us),
adorned with gems, and in a costly dress, having only a wand in
her hand, and a rich gold ring at the top of it, could travel from
one end of the kingdom to the other, without the least chance of
robbery, or even *abduction*, on the way. So excellent was the police of Brian Boromhe, and, still better, so moral and well-behaved
were his subjects!

The only thing that seems to have been out of order among the
ancient Irish was their alphabet, in which the letter A had been
unaccountably deposed from its supremacy to make way for B.[1]
Whether the ROCKS had any hand in this revolutionary movement
among the letters does not appear; but Hutcheson (in his *Dé-
fence*, etc.) in a great degree exculpates them from such a suspi-
cion, being of opinion that the colony which first imported the
alphabet into Ireland, had come away with it from Phœnicia rather
in a hurry, before the point of precedence between A and B was
properly settled.

With respect to the origin of the family name, ROCK, antiquarians and etymologists are a good deal puzzled. An idea exists in
certain quarters that the letters of which it is composed are merely
initials, and contain a prophetic announcement of the high destiny
that awaits, at some time or other, that celebrated gentleman,
Mr. Roger O'Connor, being, as they fill up the initials, the following awful words,—*R*oger *O C*onnor, *K*ing!

Others perceive in the name an indication of the design of the
Papists to establish their own religion in Ireland, through the
instrumentality of Captain ROCK, and quote in support of this con-
jecture the sacred text—"On this *Rock* I will build my church;"
while others, not less learned, are persuaded that the name has
some connexion with the *Saxum Jacobi*, or Stone of Jacob, which
(according to Mr. Hamilton, who has written to prove that the
Irish are Jews) was brought from Egypt to Ireland, some time before the general Exod under Moses, by a portion of the tribe of

---

[1] It appears, however, from Mr. O'Halloran, that St. Patrick acted the part of
General Monk to the alphabet, and that the restoration of A to its birth-right *is one*
of the chief achievements for which we are indebted to him.

Joseph, called Eranites, and is now under the coronation chair, in Westminster-Abbey.[1]

In support of this hypothesis (namely, that the Irish are Jews) Mr. Hamilton has produced some very striking proofs. Thus, he shows that the fine linen, mentioned in Revelations as worn by those personages who are to gain a victory over the Beast, is an evident allusion to the staple manufacture of Ireland; while the "harps" which they bear are, no less evidently, intended to represent the provincial arms of Leinster, which have been (as Mr. O'Halloran tells us) a harp, *or,* strung, *argent,* in a field *vert,* ever since the landing of Heber and Heremon in Ireland, on the 17th day of Bel, or May, in the year of the world, according to the Hebrew computation, 2736.

The Irish being thus indisputably proved to be Jews, it is to be hoped that the Irish country gentlemen (now that their estates are beginning to illustrate the doctrine of Evanescent Quantities) will, when forced to take refuge in the arms of their brethren of Israel, find them considerate and compassionate, if it were for nothing but old consanguinity's sake.

With respect to the moral character of my ancestors in the times of Ollam Fodlah and Brian Boromhe, there is no doubt that, however suppressed or modified, it must have been pretty much the same that it is at present. The Great Frederick used to say, that while the French fight for glory, the Spaniards for religion, and the English for liberty, the Irish are the only people in the world who fight *for fun;* and, however true this may be of my countrymen in general, there is no doubt of its perfect correctness as applied to the Rock Family in particular. Discord is, indeed, our natural element; like that storm-loving animal, the seal, we are comfortable only in a tempest; and the object of the following historical and biographical sketch is to show how kindly the English government has at all times consulted our taste in this particular——ministering to our love of riot through every successive reign, from the invasion of Henri II. down to the present day, so as to leave scarcely an interval during the whole six hundred years in which the Captain Rock for the time might not exclaim,

" Quæ regio in terris nostri non plena laboris?"

or, as it has been translated by one of my family :—

Through Leinster, Ulster, Connaught, Munster,
Rock's the boy to make the fun stir !

[1] " This marble chair was lent by the monarch of Ireland to Fergus, King of Scots, and it remained at Scone until the year 1296, when it was, with other regalia, carried to England by the first Edward."—*O'Halloran.*—It is said to make a remarkable noise when any of the true descendants of Milesius sit upon it.

CHAPTER II.

1172—1189.

Reign of Henry II. — Queues and Mustachios.—Attention to them by the
Legislature.—Fine for killing a mere Irishman.—The O'Driscolls expensive killing.—English and Irish cursing each other.—Apostrophe
to Tithes.

In the year 1180, and for some centuries after, if a man was caught
in Ireland with his upper lip unshaven, he was held to be no true
Englishman, and might be plundered without ceremony, or killed at
a very trifling expense.

In the year 1798, under the government of Lords Camden and
Castlereagh, if a man was caught in Dublin who had no queue, he
was held, in the same manner, to be no true Englishman, and
might be whipped, *ad libitum*, by any loyal gentleman who
had one.

This shows, at least, how steadily the rulers of Ireland have persevered in their ancient maxims of policy, and what importance may
be given to mustachios and tails by a government that will but for
six hundred years set seriously about it. In the former period, of
course the whiskers of the ROCK Familly flourished,—persecution
being to whiskers more nutritive than the best Macassar oil; and,
in the latter period, Crops, as we all know, became so formidable
as to require not only an army of twenty or thirty thousand men,
but all Lord Cornwallis's good sense and humanity, to put them
down again.

I have said that the penalty, in those times, for killing a mere
Irishman was but small. Sometimes, however, the price was higher.
Sir John Davies, in his *Historical Relations*, tells us of " one
William, the son of Roger, who, among others, was, by John
Wogan, Lord-Justice of Ireland, fined five marks for killing one
O'Driscoll [1]; "—this was an unusually extravagant mulct; and it
would be a curious research for an antiquary to inquire why the
O'Driscolls were so much more expensive killing than other people.

The following verses, adressed, I understand, to a certain personage, whose hatred of an Irishman is, at least, equal to his love of
a guinea, come nearer, perhaps, to the sum at which, in the honey-

---

[1] In the 4th of Edward II. R. de Wayleys was tried at Waterford for felo-
niously slaying John Mac Gillimorry. The prisoner confesses the fact, but pleads
that " he could not thereby commit felony ; because the deceased was a mere Irishman, and not of free blood, " etc., etc.—See the *Eleventh Address of Dr. Lucas*
on this subject.

moon of our English connexion, the life of a " *merus Hibernus* " was valued ;—

> " Oh, hadst thou lived when every Saxon clown
> First stabb'd his foe, and then paid half-a-crown ;
> With such a choice in thy well-balanced scale,
> Say, would thy avarice or thy spite prevail ? "

It was in such times, and under such laws, that my pugnacious progenitors first rose into repute, and began that career which, under the various names of *Mere Irish, Rapparees, White-boys*, etc., they have continued prosperously down to the present day.

It has usually been the policy of conquerors and colonists to blend as much as possible with the people among whom they establish themselves,—to share with them the advantage of their own institutions,—to remove all invidious distinctions that might recal the memory of their original invasion or intrusion,—in short, to sow in their new neighbourhood the seeds of future shelter and ornament, instead of perversely applying themselves to the culture of poison, and sitting down, like witches, with a plantation of night-shade around them.

Had our English conquerors adopted this ordinary policy, the respectable Family of the ROCKS might never have been heard of ; a few dozen rebellions would have been lost to the page of history ; and Archbishop Magee would not, perhaps, at this moment, have been throwing six millions of people into convulsions with an antithesis [1].

The English, it is evident, from the very first, disdained to owe any thing to love or good will in the " *inamabile regnum* " which they established among us, and Sir J. Davies, already quoted (with a candour like that of more modern functionaries, who acknowledge the misrule of every government but their own, and grant that, up to the precise moment when they come into power, all was wrong), thus briefly describes the policy that prevailed during the first three hundred and fifty years of British domination in Ireland :—" It was certainly a great defect in the civil policy of Ireland, that, for the space of three hundred and fifty years, at least, after the conquest first attempted, the English laws were not communicated to its people, nor the benefit or protection thereof allowed them ; for, as long as they were out of the protection of the laws, so as every

---

[1] See the celebrated Charge of this prelate, where, after asserting that the Presbyterians have a Religion without a Church, his Grace balances the antithesis, by adding that the Catholics have " a Church *without a Religion* "—thus nullifying, at one touch of his archiepiscopal pen, the creed of not only six-sevenths of his fellow-countrymen, but of the great majority of the whole Christian world. Never did a figure of speech produce a more lively sensation.

Englishman might oppress, spoil, and kill them without control, how was it possible they should be other than outlaws, and enemies to the crown of England?"

As, since the Reformation, a difference of creeds has been one of the chief points in that game of discord at which the government and the Rock family play so indefatigably together, it may be supposed that, at the period of which I am speaking, the agreement of both parties in the same belief would, at least, have narrowed the arena of dissension, and that discord being thus " at one entrance quite shut out," they would have had rather more idle time on their hands than at present.

But people, well inclined to differ, seldom find much difficulty in managing it. In the Arian controversy [1] it required but that innocent diphthong *oi* to set the whole Christian world by the ears for ages; and no mightier monosyllables than " by " and " from " have produced a schism between the Greek and Latin churches for ever.

Our English polemics, however, required no such important differences to stimulate in them the " *odium ecclesiasticum* " against their Popish brethren, but at once proceeded to burn their churches [1], and murder their priests, with as right good will as if all the letters of the alphabet had been at issue between them.

The effect of this aggression was such as might be expected, and the country soon exibited the extraordinary spectacle of two hostile altars set up by the same Faith, at which believers in the same Pope knelt down to curse each other, with no other difference in the formula of their maledictions than that one cursed in English and the other in Irish. Well might a philosophic member of the Rock family exclaim, in witnessing this phenomenon, " If such is the mode in which these pious persons *agree*, what precious sport we shall have when they *differ!* " ·

I had almost forgot to mention,—though of the utmost importance in a history of our family,—that to the occupation of Ireland by the English we are supposed to be in a great degree indebted for the first regular introduction of the blessed system of tithes. Among the bribes, by which the prelates of Ireland were induced to yield

---

[1] Tu fis dans une guerre et si triste et si longue
Périr tant de Chrétiens, *martyrs d'une diphthongue.*
                                        BOILEAU.

[1] " In Ireland it had long been a custom for the inhabitants to deposit provisions, and effects of greater value, in the churches, where they lay secure, amidst all their domestic quarrels, as in a kind of sanctuary, which it was deemed the utmost impiety to violate. But the English had no such superstitious scruples."— LELAND.

" The Irish, at length, to deprive their invaders of this resource, burnt down their own churches (as their annals express it), *in spite to the foreigners.*"—*Idem.*

obedience to the bull of Adrian, and surrender the sovereignty of their country to Henry II., was that article of reformation (as it was called), passed by the synod of Cashel, which enjoined the payment of tithes by the laity,—a mode of taxation till then, it seems, hardly known in Ireland. Mr. O'Halloran, it is true, asserts the contrary; and even represents the ancient Irish to have been such exemplary tithe-payers, that they not only contributed a tenth of their corn and cattle to the church, but threw every tenth child[1], as a make-weight into the bargain,—a species of small-tithe, by the by, which, in the present state of the population of Ireland, and the enormous wealth of the Irish church, it might not be unadvisable to restore to the parson.

Mr. O'Halloran, however, is not always to be depended upon; and, in addition to other evidence, we have lately had the expressed opinion of a learned and right reverend Roman Catholic prelate[2], that the payment of tithes, as a regular and compulsory due, may be dated from the period to which I have referred it.

Honour and praise then to the Synod of Cashel, for having planted among us this additional apple of discord, which, unlike the apples of Mr. Andrew Knight, has neither changed in character, nor degenerated in flavour; but, by the side of the Orange[3], and other wholesome fruits, still blooms in the garden of the ROCKS with undiminished strength and fertility! All hail, too, most ancient and venerable Tithes, by whatever name ye delight to be called, prædial, mixed, or personal?—long may ye flourish, with your attendant blessings of valuators, tithe-farmers, and bishops' courts, to the infinite recreation of the ROCK Family, to the honour and glory of parsons Morrit, Morgan, etc., and to the maintenance for ever of the Church Militant, as by law (and constables) established in Ireland!

---

[1] Among the pastoral customs of those happy times they used (says Dr. Milner) to baptize their children in buttermilk.

[2] See the *Vindication of the Irish Catholics*, by Bishop Doyle,—the most striking display of clerical talent and courage that has appeared among the Catholics since the days of O'Leary.

[3] " O sanctas gentes, quibus hæc nascuntur in hortis Numina!"

JUVENAL.

CHAPTER III.

1189—1509.

Period between Henry II. and Henry VIII.—The Irish partial to Justice.
—Ineffectual efforts to obtain it.—Parallel between the Barons of
Edward I. and the Orange Ascendancy.—Rebellion of the Macs and
O's.—The Rocks in Danger.—Penal Laws under Edward III.—Captain
Rock's Taste for Music.—Surprising Ingratitude and Obstinacy of the
Irish.

A SHORT review of some of the reigns that preceded the Reformation will sufficiently account for the distinguished part that
my ancestors played during the whole of that period.

My unlucky countrymen have always had a taste for justice—a
taste as inconvenient to them, situated as they have always been,
as a fancy for horse-racing would be to a Venetian.

In the reign of Edward I., that part of the native population
which came in immediate contact with the English settlements, and
which it was, therefore, a matter of the utmost importance to con-
ciliate, petitioned the King to adopt them as his subjects, and to
admit them under the shelter of the English law. They even tried
the experiment of bribing the Throne into justice. "An application
was made," says Leland, "to Ufford, the chief governor, and
eight thousand marks offered to the King, provided he would grant
the free enjoyment of the laws of England to the whole body of the
Irish inhabitants. A petition, wrung from a people tortured by the
painful feelings of oppression, in itself so just and reasonable, and
in its consequences so fair and promising, could not but be favourably received by a prince possessed with exalted ideas of policy and
government, and, where ambition did not interfere, a friend to
justice."

But, though the King was well inclined to accede to their re-
quest, and even ordered that a convention should be summoned to
take this petition into consideration, luckily for the lovers of discord and misrule his wise and benevolent intentions were not allowed to take effect. The proud Barons, to whom he had entrusted
the government of Ireland (or, in other words, the Orange Ascendancy of that day), could not so easily surrender their privilege of
oppression ¹, but, preferring victims to subjects, resolved to keep
the Irish as they were; and the arguments, or rather evasions, by

---

¹ "The great English settlers found it more for their interest that a free course
should be left to their oppressions; that many of those whose lands they coveted
should be considered as aliens; that they should be furnished for their petty wars
by arbitrary exactions; and in their rapines and massacres be freed from the ter-
rors of a rigidly impartial tribunal."—LELAND.

which they got rid of the question altogether, so closely resemble the shallow pretexts which have been played off against the claims of the Catholics in our own time, that their folly, though of so old a date, appears to us quite recent and modern, and they might have been uttered by Mr. Goulburn last week, without any breach of costume or appearance of anachronism :—"Edward was assured that an immediate compliance with his commands was not possible in *the present state of things*; that the kingdom was in too great ferment and commotion," etc. etc.—"And such pretences," adds Leland, "were sufficient, *where the aristocratic faction was so powerful.*"

Read "Orange faction" here, and you have the wisdom of our rulers, at the end of near six centuries, *in statu quo.*

The Grand Periodic Year of the Stoics, at the close of which every thing was to begin again, and the same events to be all re-acted in the same order, is, on a miniature scale, represented in the History of the English Government in Ireland—every succeeding century being but a renewed revolution of the same follies, the same crimes, and the same turbulence that disgraced the former. But "vive l'Ennemi!" say I :—whoever may suffer by such measures, Captain ROCK, at least, will prosper.

And such was the result at the period of which I am speaking. The rejection of a petition, so humble and so reasonable, was followed, as a matter of course, by one of those daring rebellions, into which the revenge of an insulted people naturally breaks forth. The M'Cartys, the O'Briens, and all the other Macs and O's [1], who have been kept upon the alert by similar causes ever since [2], flew to

---

[1] According to the following distich, the titles Mac and O are not merely what the logicians call accidents, but altogether essential to the very being and substance of an Irishman.

Per *Mac* atque O tu veros cogroscis Hibernos :
His duobus demptis, nullus Hibernus adest.

Thus translated by one of our celebrated poets.

By Mac and O,
You'll always know
True Irishmen, they say;
For if they lack
Both O and Mac,
No Irishmen are they.

[2] The system of free-quartering, which was so successful in provoking insurrection in the year 1798, is, like all our other blessings, of ancient origin. "The compendious method," says Leland, "of quartering the soldiers on the inhabitants, and leaving them to support themselves by arbitrary exactions, was adopted with alacrity and executed with rigour. Riot, rapine, massacre, and all the tremendous effects of anarchy, were the natural consequences. *Every inconsiderable party, who, under pretence of loyalty, received the king's commission to repel the*

arms under the command of a chieftain of my family, and, as the proffered *handle* of the sword had been rejected, made their inexorable masters at least feel its *edge*.

Still, such a hankering had the poor Irish after law and justice, that, about fifty years after, in the reign of Edward III., they again tried to soften the hearts of their oppressors, and "addressing themselves once more to the Throne of England, petitioned that *all those odious distinctions*, which had so long deluged the land with blood, should, at last, be abolished, and that the Irish inhabitants should be admitted to the state and privileges of English subjects."

We need not ask what was the fate of this second memorable petition. Had it succeeded Captain ROCK would not have been here to tell the story. Gibbon says, in speaking of some early action in which Mahomet was engaged, "At that moment the lance of an Arab might have changed the destinies of the world;" and it is not less true, that a stroke from the pen of Edward III. might, at this period, have changed the destinies of the ROCKS for ever.

But "Dis aliter visum est"—that spirit, which has always watched over the Anglo-Irish councils, never suffering them, in a single instance, to deviate into right, prevailed as usual, and the result was as follows:—"The petition was remitted to the Chief Governor, Darcy. He was directed to refer it to the Irish parliament, and, *as usual*, it was either clandestinely defeated, or openly rejected."

Up rose the O's and Macs again, and again did the flame of war extend as before, through Meath, Munster, and those other classic regions of turbulence, which still " live in numbers and look *green* in song;" and so weakened were the English by the hostility they had thus provoked, that (as the historian remarks) "it was only the want of concert and union among the Irish that prevented them from demolishing the whole fabric of English power."

The following laws passed during this glorious, but arbitrary reign, abundantly prove that the spirit of the Penal Code did not wait to be evoked by religious rancour[1], but was as active and virulent when both parties were Papists, as it has been since Henry VIII.

---

adversary, in some particular district, became pestilent enemies to the inhabitants. Their properties, their lives, the chastity of their families, were all exposed to these barbarians."

A historian of the Rebellion of 1798 might transfer this passage to his page with perfect truth and fitness.

[1] "In the reign of Edward III," says Leland, " pride and self-interest concurred in regarding and representing the Irish as a race utterly irreclaimable." Four hundred years after, in the time of Swift, it was the fashion, he tells us, in England, "to think and to affirm that the Irish cannot be too hardly used." A hundred years hence, perhaps, the same language will be repeated.

made it a war of creeds as well as nations.—"It was enjoined by Royal mandate that no mere Irishman should be admitted into any office or trust in any city, borough, or castle in the King's land." Again, by the parliamentary ordinance, called the Statutes of Kilkenny, it was enacted "that marriage, nurture of infants, and gossipred with the Irish should be considered and punished as high-treason;" and "it was also made highly penal to the English to permit their Irish neighbours to graze their lands, to present them to ecclesiastical benefices, or to receive them into monasteries or religious houses." Even the poetry and music of the poor Irish were proscribed, and it was made penal "to entertain their bards, who perverted the imagination by romantic tales."

In the reign of Henry IV., the Irish "Enemy" (for so the natives were styled in all legal documents) showed, naturally enough, a disposition to emigrate—but, by a refined mixture of cruelty and absurdity, which is only to be found, *genuine*, in Irish legislation, an act of parliament was passed to prevent them. Those whom the English refused to incorporate with subjects, they would yet compel to remain as rebels or as slaves. "By an act of the Irish parliament, in the eleventh year of Henry IV., it was ordained that no Irish enemy should be permitted to depart from the realm." We have heard of a bridge of gold for a flying enemy, but an act of parliament to compel him to stand his ground could only have been passed by an Irish Legislature.

This unvarying system of hostility and oppression, which had been hitherto directed only against the natives, was now extended to such descendants of the old English settlers as had adopted a more natural policy than the government, and by marriage, commerce, and other peaceful mediums, become gradually mingled with the native population[1]. Upon these, as lying most within the reach of their insolence, the new-comers of English birth particularly indulged in the most wanton tyranny; and thus not only gave birth to the distinction of an English and Irish interest, but by identifying some of the oldest English families with the letter, arrayed a new force on the side of their enemies, and gave an additional strength and respectability to rebellion.[2]

---

[1] In remarking upon this coalition, Leland sensibly and candidly remarks—"It may be doubted whether such effect could possibly have been produced, if the old natives had ever been possessed invariably and unalterably with that inveterate national aversion, to which their repeated insurrections are commonly ascribed. The solution was easy, and might have served the purposes of a selfish policy, but there are other causes equally obvious to be assigned."

[2] "English by birth and English by race were become terms of odious distinction; and every day produced violences which gradually became considerable enough to require the immediate interposition of the King."

Perfect policy, throughout!—never, in the paths of legislation, were there "*meilleurs guides pour s'égarer.*" So uniformly, too, has the same tree produced the same fruits, that, at three such distant epochs as the reigns of Henry IV., Elizabeth, and George III., we find the noble and English name of Fitzgerald "flaming in the front" of Revolt!

Among many minor points of resemblance between our popish rulers of those days and our Reformed ones of the present[1], may be counted that quick and distracting change of Lieutenantcies succeeding one another like the groupes of a magic lantern, each in its separate frame or slider, each differing from its predecessor in plans and opinions, and thus rendering the government, like Penelope's web, a mere system of doing and undoing.

The account given by Spenser of this motley procession of Lord Lieutenants is like a picture painted yesterday—so fresh are all its colours and so living its likenesses. "The governors (says he) are usually envious of one another's greater glory, which if they would seek to excel by better government, it would be a most laudable emulation. But they doe quite otherwise. For this is the common order of them, that who cometh next in place will not follow that course of government which his predecessors held, either for disdane of himself, or doubt to have his doings drowned in another man's praise, but will straight take a way quite contrary to the former: *as if the former thought by keeping under the Irish to reform them, the next, by discountenancing the English, will curry favour with the Irish, and so make his government seem plausible, as having the Irish at his command. But he that comes after will perhaps follow neither the one nor the other, but will dandle the one and the other in such sort, as he will sucke sweet out of them both and leave bitternesse to the poor country.*"

Our modern plan, it must be confessed, improves upon the

---

[1] There is no end to the resemblances between the two periods. The following passage is not more applicable to the English colonists of those days, than to the English capitalists of the present: "Such conceptions had been formed of the state of Ireland and the disorders of its inhabitants that even they who had received Irish grants could neither be persuaded to repair thither, nor to send any persons to the custody of their lands, notwithstanding the reiterated edicts of the King."

Again, in the reign of Henry V.—"*The king's personal appearance in Ireland is most earnestly entreated to save his people from destruction.*" And, in the same reign,—"the *infection of party* and jealousy spread through all orders, and *was caught even by the Clergy, who should have restrained and moderated it.*" The following coincidence is still more curious:—"*Talbot* conducted the government with the greater ease, *as he seems to have resigned himself entirely to the reigning* faction."

Thus, "*semper eadem*" (and generally according to the *Irish* translation of it "worse and worse,") is destined to be the motto of Ireland to the end of time.

distraction of this, for not only have we Governors of discordant politics succeeding each other, but every new Governor is provided with a Secretary to differ with him for the time being, and both receive their instructions from a Cabinet, not one member of which agrees with another. If this is not sounding the pitch-pipe of discord, Captain Rock has no ear for that kind of music.

I have thus selected, cursorily and at random, a few features of the reigns preceding the Reformation, in order to show what good use was made of those three or four hundred years, in attaching the Irish people to their English governors; and by what a gentle course of alteratives they were prepared for the inoculation of a new religion, which was now about to be attempted upon them by the same skilful and friendly hands.

Henry the VIIth appears to have been the first monarch to whom it occurred, that matters were not managed exactly as they ought in this part of his dominions; and we find him—with a simplicity, which is still fresh and youthful among our rulers—expressing his *surprise* that "his subjects of this land should be so prone to faction and rebellion, and that so little advantage had been hitherto derived from the acquisitions of his predecessors, notwithstanding the fruitfulness and natural advantages of Ireland."

Surprising, indeed, that a policy such as we have been describing should not have converted the whole country into a perfect Atalantis of happiness.—Should not have made it like the imaginary island of Sir Thomas More, where "*tota insula velut una familia est!*"—most stubborn, truly, and ungrateful must that people be, upon whom, up to the very hour in which I write, such a long and unvarying course of penal laws, confiscations, and Insurrection Acts has been tried, without making them, in the least degree, in love with their rulers!

Heloisa tells her tutor, Abelard, that the correction which he inflicted upon her only increased the ardour of her affection for him;—but bayonets and hemp are no such "*amoris stimuli.*"

One more characteristic anecdote of those times, and I have done. At the battle of Knocktow, in the reign of Henry VII., when that remarkable man, the Earl of Kildare, assisted by the great O'Neal and other Irish chiefs, gained a victory over Clanricard of Connaught, most important to the English Government, Lord Gormanstown, after the battle, in the first insolence of success, said, turning to the Earl of Kildare, "we have slaughtered our enemies, but, to complete the good deed, we must proceed yet further, and—cut the throats of those Irish of our own party." [1]

Who can wonder that the Rock Family were active in those times?

[1] Leland gives this anecdote on the authority of an Englishman.

CHAPTER IV.

1509—1553.

Reigns of Henry VIII. and Edward VI.—Gentle methods of introducing
the Reformation into Ireland.—Parallel between Bishop Bale and
Archbishop Magee.—Unchangeableness of the Irish.—Versatility of
the English.

HENRY the Eighth, who was as fond of theology as of dancing,[1]
executed various *pirouettes* in the former line, through which he,
rather unreasonably, compelled the whole nation to follow him;
and, difficult as it was to keep pace with his changes, either as
believer, author, or husband, or know which of his creeds he
wished to be maintained, which of his books he wished to be
believed, or which of his wives he wished *not* to be beheaded, the
people of England, to do them justice, obeyed every signal of his
caprice with a suppleness quite wonderful, and danced the hays
with their monarch and his unfortunate wives through every variety
of mystery and murder, into which Thomas Aquinas and the execu-
tioner could lead them.

But they, upon whom a blessing falls, have no right to be particular as to the source from whence it comes; and though (as Gray
with infinite gallantry expresses it)

> 'Twas Love that taught this monarch to be wise, .
> And Gospel light first beam'd from Boleyn's eyes—

though the Faith, thus derived, has preserved, ever since, the
"*varium semper et mutabile*" character of its source, yet that
it *was* a blessing to England and her liberties, even Captain ROCK—
all Papist as he is—will not deny[2]. The very variety and mutable-
ness of English Protestantism is congenial with the spirit of Civil
Liberty, which delights to follow the branching rivulets of opinion,
and has always found her harvests most rich where these meander-
ing streams most freely circulate.

[1] " Sir W. Molyneux (says Lloyd) got in with King Henry the Eighth, by a
discourse out of Aquinas in the morning, and a dance at night."—*State Worthies.*

[2] I beg to direct the attention of the reader to the remarkable liberality here
displayed by Captain ROCK. I must say, indeed, that in the course of my short
acquaintance with the Captain, I found him, upon all subjects (except that of
Church property), a perfect gentleman—resembling, in this respect, most of his
brother-heroes, among whom there is scarcely one,

> Qui, s'il ne violoit, voloit, tuoit, brûloit,
> Ne fût assez bonne personne.   EDITOR.

But the Irish were not to be dragooned into blessings. Strongly attached as they have ever been to their ancient faith and ancient institutions, it would have required either a docility under the rod of despotism, which is one of the faults most rarely imputed to them, or a long course of confidence in the wisdom and good intention of their rulers, which is still, unluckily, a desideratum in their hearts —to have weaned them from a religion, so interwoven with all their feelings and recollections. Proffered even by the most friendly hand, the boon of Reformation would have been slowly, if at all, accepted; but, preached from the mouths of the same race, whose cry had never been aught but "Death to the Irish!" and accompanied by all that apparatus of persecution, with which Laws and Religion have ever been surrounded in Ireland, is it wonderful that the boon should have been fiercely and at once rejected? is it wonderful that a continuance of the same persecuting policy, which made us spurn, without inquiry, the creed of our oppressors *then*, should have kept us good Catholics and bad subjects ever since?

As a specimen of the gentle arts by which the new religion was recommended to the people, read what follows :—"Under pretence of obeying the orders of state, they seized all the most valuable furniture of the churches, which they exposed to sale without decency or reserve. The Irish annalists pathetically describe the garrison of Athlone issuing forth with a barbarous and heathen fury, and pillaging the famous church of Clonmacnoise, tearing away the most inoffensive ornaments, so as to leave the shrine of their favourite Saint Kieran a hideous monument of sacrilege '."

The venerable crozier of St. Patrick, too, which, even in the present enlightened times, would be viewed, I fear, with more genuine homage than all the assembled croziers and mitres of the whole Protestant bench of Ireland, was, by the Vandal reformers of that period, insultingly committed to the flames.

Conciliation, indeed, seems to have been as well understood then as it is at present; and the Prelate selected in the reign of Edward VI. to smooth the way to the establishment of the Protestant Religion in Ireland, appears to have transmitted his mantle to that mild and tolerant Archbishop who is at present so actively employed in maintaining it there.

Raised from an obscure origin by his talents and learning, Bale, the Bishop of Ossory, on becoming a Lord of the Church aristocracy, assumed the arrogance of station as a substitute for the pride of birth, and, mistaking violence of temper for religious zeal, employed the "live coals from the altar" in kindling around him dissension and

' Leland.

revenge. " Even the weak among the new-reformed (says the historian) were terrified; and the Romish party held this spirited and turbulent enemy in the utmost abhorrence. He insulted the prejudices of the people without reserve or caution, and, during the short period of his residence in Ireland lived in a continual state of fear and persecution."

If a Charioteer of this temper was, like Phaeton, but ill qualified to guide the car of the New Light up the steep ascent of its "prima via," how doubly perilous is the guidance of such a rash hand now, when

Ultima via *prona* est, et eget moderamine certo,—OVID.

The obstinate perseverance of the Irish in their old belief, is not, perhaps, more remarkable than the readiness with which the people of England veered about from one religion to another, during the three reigns that succeeded the Reformation [1].

It is a curious proof of the utter indifference with which persons in authority viewed those great changes of religion, that Sir Antony Saintleger, who had been entrusted with the government of Ireland, when the new regulations of divine worship were to be established, in the reign of Edward, was again made deputy, in the time of Mary, when these same regulations were to be all abolished!

Bacon seems to think that a versatile disposition gains as much in happiness as it loses in dignity [2]—and, certainly, whatever dignity Ireland may have maintained by adhering so steadily to her ancient faith, the happiness that results from versatility is all on the side of England.

[1] Lloyd describes them, during the interval between Mary's accession and her first parliament, as, "like the Jewish children after the captivity, speaking a middle language between Hebrew and Ashdod."—See his *State Worthies,* in which we find recorded a number of those eminent, and, no doubt, excellent persons, who contrived, notwithstanding the very opposite interests that prevailed in the reigns of Henry, Edward, Mary, and Elizabeth, to hold situations of trust under all these sovereigns.

Nor was it only politicians that exhibited this convenient flexibility—the great reformer Latimer changed his opinion no less than eight different times.—See Lingard, vol. vii. p. 269. "Cranmer's faith (says Mr. Brodie) was continually changing. He at one time as furiously persecuted those who denied transubstantiation as ever he did any other imputed heresy, and was long a stickler for pilgrimages, purgatory," etc.—*History of the British Empire.*

In the parliament convened in Ireland, upon the accession of Elizabeth, "Most of the temporal lords (says Leland) were those whose descendants, even to our own days, continue firmly attached to the Romish communion; *but far the greater part of the prelates were such as quietly enjoyed their sees by conforming occasionally to different modes of religion.*"

[2] Ingenia gravia et solennia et *mutare nescia* plus plerumque habeant dignitatis quam felicitatis.—*De Augment. Scient.*

CHAPTER V.

1553—1558.

Reign of Mary.—Lord Eldon and the Duke of Wellington, Papists.—
Captain Rock, a Protestant.—Anecdote of Lord C——n.—Peace and
Tolerance, for once, in Ireland.—Eradicating the Cockle.—Burnings
on both sides.

THE Irish were, as we have seen, from the very first, declared
" enemies " by the English law, and it is the only declaration of the
English law by which they have very cordially abided ever since. So
invariably, indeed, has England taught them to consider *their* interests as the very antipodes of *hers*, that had the restoration of
Popery in Mary's time been permanent, it would have required
but a good course of persecuting Popish Lord Lieutenants, to convert the great mass of the Irish nation to Protestantism.

What a change would this have produced! Six millions of Luther-
ans might now have been the petitioning body – the idolatry of the
Corporation of Dublin would have been lavished upon Saint Bridget,
instead of King William—some Jesuit, instead of Lord Eldon, some
crusader, instead of the Duke of Wellington, might have been prof-
fering their swords and counsels against the cause of Religious Liberty ; and, to crown all, Captain ROCK, for want of better, might
have been forced to put up with the Reformed Creed, and endeavoured to make himself no less troublesome as a Protestant, than, he
flatters himself, he is now as a Papist.

Such is the world, and on such chances depend the wisdom and
station of the men who constitute it! But, luckily for England, the
Reformation triumphed under Elizabeth, and luckily for Captain
ROCK, all possible means were taken to render it odious and intolerable in Ireland.

According to the usual rule of contrariety between the two countries, the reign of Mary, which was attended with such horrors in
England, is almost the only interval of peace and quietness that the
annals of my ancestors exhibit in Ireland. Some local fighting, it is
true, took place among my relatives the O'Briens, O'Neals, etc.,
but little more than was absolutely necessary to keep their hands in
practice against a change of administration.

The last Lord C——n, upon being found one day by a friend,
practising with his sword against the wainscoat before dinner, and
being asked the reason of his assiduity at this exercise, answered,
" I have some company to-day that I expect to quarrel with "—
and pretty much in the same manner the members of my family are
obliged occasionally to rehearse, even in their moments of tranquil-

lity, for the reception of any new guests that may be sent them , in the shape of governors, from England.

With the exception, however, of these trifling interruptions, both government and people were at peace during the whole of this reign; and it is worthy of remark, that the only period in which the Irish have been left the *unmolested* exercise of their religion , was a period of perfect tranquillity and tolerance—such freedom from persecution being enjoyed at this time, that, according to Ware, " several English families, friends to the Reformation, fled to Ireland, and there enjoyed their opinions and worship without notice or molestation : "—this, too, during the bloody reign of Queen Mary.! Will our rulers *never* read History ?

The pestilent bigotry with which England was infected after the Reformation has been represented as exclusively a *Catholic* disease, and for no other purpose than to justify Protestants in appropriating all the remains of the virus to themselves. Luckily, however, the lion has taken his turn to be painter. Dr. Lingard, an able Catholic divine, has established beyond doubt the melancholy fact , that the spirit of persecution was equally busy on both sides, and that Cranmer was the author of that Penal Code ¹ against Heresy, under which himself and others were so cruelly sacrificed afterwards.

The intolerant principle of " eradicating the cockle " and " cutting out the gangrene ," was common to the professors of both creeds—the only difference was, as to the extent to which this principle was put into practice : and, even reducing the question thus to a mere summing-up of victims, when we have taken into account the Anabaptists and Unitarians, burned in the time of Edward VI. and Elizabeth, together with the long list of Catholics, who , under various pretences, were racked and executed during the latter reign, it will leave a balance , in favour of Protestant tolerance ², by no

---

¹ " Edward died before this code had obtained the sanction of the legislature: by the accession of Mary , the power of the sword passed from the hands of one religious party to those of the other ; and within a short time Cranmer and his associates perished in the flames which they had prepared to kindle for the destruction of their opponents."—LINGARD, vol. vii. p. 259.

ᴬ Mr. Southey , indeed, acknowledges that Cranmer, when he brought Lambert to the stake, " with circumstances of peculiar barbarity," believed the corporal presence, " and held also the atrocious opinion, that death by fire was the just and appropriate punishment for heresy. This (he adds) plainly appeared afterwards in a case wherein he was deeply criminal."

With all this candour , however , Mr. Southey is but a partial martyrologist. While he devotes whole pages to the sufferings of almost every victim of Queen Mary, he thus despatches a poor Dutchman who was burned in the reign of Edward :—" There were some, also, who abjured Arian and Socinian opinions; but for the former a Dutchman suffered at the stake."—*Book of the Church.*

² In Mr. Southey's *Book of the Church* we find a striking proof of the pertinacity

means considerable enough to be looked back to with pride ; particularly if this small difference in the amount of bigotry *then*, is to be made a pretext by the stronger party *now*, for monopolizing the whole bigotry to itself, in future.

CHAPTER VI.

1558—1603.

Reign of Elizabeth.—Hibernia pacified.—Bon-mot of Queen Elizabeth. — Famine a Means of quieting Ireland.—Liberal Policy of England.— Kings of Egypt.—Fish-adorers and Dog-worshippers.—One of my Ancestors distinguished in the Rebellious Line.—Precious Relic in the Possession of my Family.

THE plan of pacifying Ireland by exterminating the Irish—the only feasible one that has yet been attempted—was tried, on a grand scale, during the reign of Elizabeth; and had so nearly succeeded, that under the government of lord Gray, the Queen was assured that " little was left in Ireland for her majesty to reign over but carcasses and ashes '." So satisfied, too, with the result of his mission was another of her agents in this work of desolation, that the record which he has left behind him of his sanguinary exploits is entitled "Pacata Hibernia," or " Hibernia pacified."

Hibernia pacified! alas, alas, could the shade of Sir G. Carew but once more hover over his own region of Munster, he would find that a new edition of his work of Pacification is much wanted — he would find that though the same peacemakers, Slaughter and Persecution, have been tried under almost every government since his time, the grand object is still unaccomplished—the Temple of the Anglo-Irish Janus (that " forma biceps ") lies as open as ever.

As I am not writing a History of the English power in Ireland, but merely tracking its course by hasty glimpses, and pointing out a few footmarks of the Hercules of despotism, from which the rest

---

with which falsehoods are persevered in for the maintenance of the good old cause of bigotry. In the very farce of Dr. Lingard's complete exposure of the absurd fiction relative to Gardner's death, this gentleman has gravely re-stated the whole tale as authentic.

' When the garrison of Smerwick, in Kerry, surrendered, upon mercy, to Lord Deputy Gray, he ordered upwards of seven hundred of them to be put to the sword or hanged. "Wingfield was commissioned to disarm them; and, when this service was performed, an English company was sent into the fort, and the garrison was butchered in cold blood: nor is it without pain (adds Leland), that we find a service so horrid and detestable committed to Sir Walter Raleigh."

For this and other such services, Sir Walter Raleigh had forty thousand acres of land bestowed upon him in the county of Cork, which he afterwards sold to Richard, first Earl of Cork.

of his colossal proportions may be estimated, I shall content myself
with selecting from the long reign of Elizabeth a trait or two most
characteristic of her general policy—or, rather, of the policy of those
employed by her; as that queen herself would have been far too wise,
had her attention been fairly directed to the subject[1], to turn thus
into a wilderness what nature meant for a garden, or make Famine
and Devastation the hand-maids of her power. There is a memorable saying of hers, preserved by Camden, which not only shows
how feelingly she was aware of the perverse wickedness of the system pursued under her name, but contains as bitter a comment on
the whole course of policy towards this country as the most virulent
United Irishman ever dared to utter.—" Alas (said she, on receiving
some representation of grievances from Ireland), how I fear lest it
be objected to us, as it was to Tiberius by Bato :—*You, you it is
that are in fault, who have committed your flocks not to shep-
herds but to wolves?*"

And now for our specimens of the policy of this reign. Let the poet
Spenser, in the first place, describe the frightful state of desolation
brought upon the people of Munster, by a war into which their
leader, the Earl of Desmond, was driven by the cupidity of the
chief Governors, who had long looked on his immense possessions
with a wishful eye[2], and, thinking him too tempting, as an enemy,
to be long suffered to remain a friend (as he himself expresses it),
" wrung him into undutifulness." — " Notwithstanding, " says

---

[1] On more than one occasion she endeavoured to introduce measures of conciliation and justice; but, in the intoxication of unlimited power, her Deputies
were incapable of either. Even when they affected to put " her Majesty's merciful
orders" into execution, the terms of pardon which they offered were but new de-
vices of cruelty. Lord Mountjoy (as we are told by his secretary Moryson) never
received any to mercy but such as had drawn blood of their fellow-rebels. " Thus, "
says he, " M'Mahon and M'Artmoyle offered to submit, *but neither could be received without the other's head.*"

Yet could this Lord Mountjoy write, as plausibly as any of our modern Secretaries speak, on the expediency of a more humane and tolerant policy. Thus, in
a letter to the Lords of the Council, he says—"All the Irish that are now obstinate, are so only out of their diffidence to be safe in any forgiveness; and, though
they are weary of the war, they are unwilling to have it ended, for fear lest, upon
a peace, there would come a severe reformation of religion. *They have the ancient
swelling and desire of liberty in their countrymen* to work upon—their fear to be
rooted out, and *generally all over the kingdom their fear of a persecution for
religion;* the least of which alone has been many times sufficient to drive the best
and most quiet states into sudden confusion."

[2] Elizabeth knew the art of turning Irish rebellions to account full as well as
any of her successors. " Be not dismayed," she said, upon hearing that O'Neal
meditated some designs against her government; " *tell my friends, if he arise,
it will turn to their advantage;* there will be estates for them who want."—LELAND,
p. 238.

Spenser, " that the same was a most riche and plentiful country, yet, ere one year and a half, they were brought to such wretchedness, as that any stony heart wou'd rue the same. Out of every corner of the woods and glynns they came creeping forth upon their hands, for their legs could not bear them ; they looked like anatomies of death ; they spake like ghosts crying out of their graves ; they did eat the dead carrions, happy where they could find them, yea, and one another soon after ; insomuch , as the very carcasses they spared not to scrape out of their graves, and if they found a plot of water-cresses or shamrocks , there they flocked as to a feast for the time, yet not able to continue there withal , that in short space there was none almost left , and a most populous and plentiful country suddenly left void of man and beast [1]. "

The authors of this calamity reaped from it the expected fruits. Five hundred and seventy-four thousand six hundred and twenty-eight acres were forfeited to the Crown , and distributed among Englishmen.

As famine had succeeded so well in Munster, it was adopted systematically in Leinster and Ulster ; and that death which Homer pronounces to be the most miserable that man can die, was now prescribed and administered universally as a panacea for all the evils of Ireland. " The soldiers ," as we learn from Moryson, " encouraged by the example of their officers, every where cut down the standing corn with their swords, and devised every means to deprive the wretched inhabitants of all the necessaries of life. Famine was judged the speediest and most effectual means of reducing them. The like expedient was practised in the northern provinces. The governor of Carrickfergus, Sir Arthur Chichester, issued from his quarters, and for twenty miles round reduced the country to a desert. Sir Samuel Bagnal, with the garrison of Newry proceeded with the same severity, and laid waste all the adjacent lands."

Such was the executive part of the measures of Elizabeth's ministers.—Let us now lift the curtain of her Councils, and see what was passing there.

It appears from the letters of Sir H. Sidney and Sir J. Perrot [2]

---

[1] *State of Ireland.*

[2] It will be perceived that throughout my brief review of the measures of England towards Ireland , I have relied almost exclusively upon English authorities, without availing myself either of the dreadful details of the Irish annalists , the high-coloured statements of the over-Catholic O'Sullivan , or even those comments full of true Irish feeling , by which honest Curry, in his valuable work on the Civil Wars of Ireland , brings out into stronger light and relief the frightful enormities which his pen has grouped together.

Leland , the only Irish authority on which I have rested, was sufficiently pro-

(who, to do them justice, speak of such conduct with the horror it desserves), that when the death of the earl of Desmond, and the supppession of his adherents, had left an interval of tranquillity which it was proposed to take advantage of, for the long-desired purpose of introducing a system of justice and liberal policy into Ireland, the counsellors of Elizabeth opposed themselves to this humane design, and did not blush to assign the following reasons for their opposition: — " Should we exert ourselves, " said they, " in reducing this country to order and civility, it must soòn acquire power, consequence, and riches. The inhabitants will be thus alienated from England; they will cast themselves into the arms of some foreign power, or perhaps erect themselves into an independent and separate State. *Let us rather connive at their disorders;* for a weak and disordered people never can attempt to detach themselves from the crown of England."

This policy was not new in the history of nations. Diodorus Siculus tells us, that the ancient Kings of Egypt kept alive the spirit of religious dissensions among their subjects, as the best means of preventing a combination against their own tyranny—well knowing, that as long as a Dog-worshipper of Cynopolis was ready to cut the throat of a Fish-adorer of Oxyrynchus, there would be no fear of any rational concord in the cause of liberty among such people. Accordingly, at one time, by giving superior privileges to the Dog establishment—at another, by mortifying the canine ascendancy, and even affecting an inclination to bring Fish-worship into fashion, they contrived to cherish such a deadly animosity between these two respectable creeds, that when the Romans, who took somewhat more sensible views of such matters, became masters of Egypt, it required (as Plutarch tells us) the strongest and most skilful interposition of their authority, to put down both Dog and Fish together —or, at least, by removing all distinctions between them, to render their worship a matter of as little consequence as they were themselves.

Never had the ROCKS a fairer harvest of riot than during this most productive reign. One of my ancestors, who lived and battled through the whole of it, has transmitted to his descendants the high and illustrious distinction, of having been personally engaged in no less than forty rebellions—making within five of the number of years that good Queen Bess (as he well might call her) reigned —to say nothing of a multitude of episodical insurrections, of a lighter nature, with which he amused his summer months.

tected against any undue partiality to his country by a Fellowship in the University of Dublin, a Prebend in St. Patrick's Cathedral, and a Chaplaincy at the Castle—all good securities against political heterodoxy.

This great ornament of our family (who appears to have been a most polyonymous, or rather polyomichronymous person, being christened O'Brien, O'Murtagh, O'Laughlin, O'Shane, etc.) was one of the worthies selected by the great Tirone, Prince of Ulster, to accompany him in his celebrated pilgrimage to the Holy Cross of Tipperary. He was also at the battle of the Pass of Plumes, where the gay young soldiers of the Earl of Essex were plucked, like fowls, by the brave rebel O'Moore—and one of those Plumes (supposed to be that which he took on the occasion) is still preserved as a relic in the ROCK Family.

CHAPTER VII.

1603—1625.

Reign of James I.—Suspected of not being a Bigot.—Declares by Proclamation that he is.—First Operations of the Law in Ireland.—Epigram. .—Seven Counties swept into the Treasury.—Extraordinary Tranquillity of my Family.—Fragment of an Ode to Riot, by a Rock on the Peace Establishment.

IT is an awful thing when an absolute monarch turns author. Henry VIII. would have been perilous handling for a critic; and a controversialist, who can say, like James, "for the present I have one of that Jesuitical order in prison, who hath face enough to maintain such doctrine," is, to say the least of him, a disconcerting antagonist.

From the following passages, in one of his speeches, it will be perceived how little this Royal author cared for reviewers,—even for reviewers of the Satanic school, which must be as formidable, I presume, in criticism, as its fellow school is in poetry :—"I confess I am loath to hang a priest only for religion-sake, and saying mass; but if he refuses to take the oath of allegiance (which, *let the pope and all the devils in hell say what they will, yet as you find by my book*, is merely civil), those that so refuse the oath, and are polypragmatic, I leave them to the law."

That the theological quibbles of this vain pedant should have puzzled the Catholics of Ireland into a belief that he meant to favour their religion, is not at all surprising [1]. He had also made them promises, before his accession to the throne, which they continued most loyally to put their trust in, long after he had violated them all,—a prince's promise being that kind of convenient talisman,

[1] They ought, however, to have been much sooner undeceived, for one of his first most gracious proclamations was to order a general gaol delivery, with the special exception of "murderers and papists."

3

which may be broken over and over, without, in the least degree,
losing its charm.

It is true King James gave fair notice of his perfidy, and was so
far honester than some other princes [1] ; for though, like them, he
availed himself of the discontent and hopes of the Catholics, to em-
barrass the measures of the reign which had preceded his own, yet
did he not, like them, attempt to carry the deceit any further, or
to keep hopes alive which it was his secret intention to blast; but
thus, by regular Proclamation, announced to his dupes the mistake
they had been under in having the least reliance upon him :—
"Whereas, his majesty is informed that his subjects of Ireland
have been deceived by a false report that his majesty was disposed
to allow them liberty of conscience and the free choice of a religion :
he hereby declares to his beloved subjects of Ireland, that he will
not admit any such liberty of conscience as they were made to
expect by such report, [2]" etc., etc.

And here, at least, his majesty kept his word. The exercise of
their religion was strictly forbidden,—their priests were banished,
and severe penalties inflicted on such as should harbour or entertain
them. All Catholics were obliged to assist at the Protestant church
service every Sunday and holiday; and thus they, who had been
called "imps of Antichrist," etc. for listening to a Latin mass
which they did not understand, were now forced to listen to an
English liturgy, which they, being Irish, understood quite as little [3].
By a refinement of cruelty, too, Roman Catholics of condition were
appointed by the state, under the name of Inquisitors, to watch,
and inform against those of their own communion who did not frequent the protestant churches on the days appointed; and if, through
any scruple of pride or conscience, they neglected or refused this
degrading duty, they were heavily fined and condemned to a long
imprisonment.

"Where's your religion, and be d——d to you?" says a pious
gentleman in one of Cumberland's plays; and much in the same

---

[1] " Certi nomini (says Boccalini, when he wishes not to be supposed to mean
living kings) del tempo antico, dei quali oggidi si è perduta la razza."

[2] Curry.

[3] Nothing is new in Ireland. Even the Bible Society plan seems to have been
tried upon the persecuted and confiscated Irish of those times.

"It was ordered that the Bible and common-prayer book should be translated
into the Irish language, which was done: and every parish-church was obliged to
pay ten shillings for an Irish Bible, when not one amongst a hundred could read
or understand it. And therefore an Irish protestant bishop did laugh at this strange
kind of alteration, and said to some of his friends, 'In Queen Elisabeth's time we
had English bibles and Irish ministers, but now we have ministers out of England,
and Irish bibles with them.' "—*Theatre of Cath. and Protest. Religion.*

sort of edifying style was the reformed religion first insinuated into the hearts of the Irish.

Another amiable feature in this reign was that system of legalized plunder, which so barefacedly flourished throughout the whole of it; and what Fielding has said, in prose, of the law, is equally true in rhyme of the government at this period :—

> The Irish had long made a deuce of a clatter,
>   And wrangled and fought about *meum* and *tuum*,
> Till England stept in, and decided the matter, .
>   By kindly converting it all into *suum*.

After some centuries of hints from the people themselves, it was at last found out by the attorney-general of King James [1], that my countrymen were by nature fond of Law and Justice; but as both together would have been too much for their unenlightened minds, it was so contrived as to give them the former without the latter; and it is a curious proof of the "*amari aliquid,*" which has always mingled with even the benefits we have received from England, that the first use made of the English law, on its first regular introduction into Ireland, was to rob thousands of the unfortunate natives of their property.

. . Under the pretence of a judicial inquiry into defective titles, a system of spoliation was established throughout the whole country, and the possessions of every man placed at the mercy of any creature of the crown, who could detect a flaw or failure in his tenure [2]— to ensure the certainty of which result, all juries, who refused to find a title in the king, were censured in the castle-chamber, and committed to prison.

In one case, a whole county was swept into the treasury by this process. "In the year 1611, on the seizure of the county of Wexford, when, upon a commission to inquire out his majesty's title to the county, the jury offered their verdict of *ignoramus* to the

---

[1] "No nation," (says Sir John Davies), "love equal and impartial justice more than the Irish." Lord Coke, too, gives the same character of them; and adds, "which virtue must necessarily be accompanied by many others." The first circuit of the judges into the northern province is thus described by Sir John Davies, who was one of them :—" Though somewhat distasteful to the Irish lords, it was most welcome to the common people, who albeit they were rude and barbarous, yet did they quickly apprehend the difference between the tyranny and oppression under which they had lived before, and the just government and protection which we *promised* unto them for the time to come."

[2] "Discoverers were every where busily employed in finding out flaws in men's titles to their estates "—LELAND. "There are not wanting proofs of the most iniquitous practices, of hardened cruelty, of vile perjury, and scandalous subornation, employed to despoil the fair and unoffending proprietor of his inheritance.—*Idem.*

king's title, the commissioners refused to accept it, and bound the jury to appear before them in the exchequer-court, where, when five of them still refused to find the title in the king, the commissioners committed them to prison. "With the same regard to justice, six entire counties of Ulster, under the pretence of a conspiracy, which (for once, in Ireland) did not exist, were forfeited, "at one fell swoop," to the crown.

Lucian tells us, that Mercury was hardly out of his cradle before he took to thieving: and it cannot be denied that the infancy of the law among us was distinguished by a similar preciousness of talent.

Why, then, were my countrymen so quiet during this reign? and how did it happen that under such genial influence of persecution and robbery, the Rocks did not flourish with more than wonted luxuriance?

This is a problem which has puzzled historians [1]. Mr. O'Halloran considers it to have been a matter of sentiment. "King James," he says, "was a descendant of our great ancestor Milesius; and therefore (like the Irishman lately, who was nearly murdered on Saint Patrick's day, but forgave his assailant 'in honour of the saint,') we bore it all quietly in honour of Milesius."

Sir John Davies takes a different view of the matter, and is of opinion that " braying people, as it were, in a mortar with sword and pestilence," is the only way to make them peaceable and comfortable. "Whereupon," says this right-thinking attorney-general, " the multitude being brayed, as it were, in a mortar with sword, famine, and pestilence together, submitted themselves to the English government; received the laws and magistrates, and most gladly embraced King James's pardon and peace in all parts of the realm *with demonstrations of joy and comfort.*"

How little, at all times, have the Irish been aware, that it was solely to produce "demonstrations of joy and comfort" that this process of braying in a mortar has so frequently been tried upon them.—"*Felices, sua si bona norint!*"

Whatever may have been the cause of this preternatural tranquillity, it is certain that it did exist to such an unaccountable degree, that the mock-conspiracy already alluded to, and a short burst of rebellion under a gentleman, whom Hume introduces to us by the foreign name of Odogartie, but who turns out (like little Flanigan disguised in "the blue and gold") to be no other than simple

---

[1] "The old Irish lords," says LELAND, in endeavouring to account for this tranquillity, "were now deeply impressed with the miseries of Tyrone's rebellion, their power and consequence diminished, without arms to furnish the remains of their followers at home, and without hopes of succour from abroad."

Mr. O'Dogherty, were the only signs of life exhibited by my ancestors, through the whole of this penal and oppressive reign.

May it not have been the management of Parliaments (a game at which both court and country were now, for the first time, learning to play) that a good deal diverted the attention of the people from more violent modes of asserting their rights?

This experiment, like the beginnings of steam navigation, was perilous, and accordingly the boiler exploded in the following reign. But, even at this early period, the use that might be made of such a machine against the people was clearly perceived, and the first rude essays of our political engineers in this line, if not instructive, are at least amusing. Thus, in order to procure a majority[1] for those penal statutes which were proposed in the Irish parliament of 1613, a number of new boroughs were hastily created, to which attorneys' clerks, and some of the servants of the lord deputy were elected; and when a representation of this grievance, among others, was made to James, his kingly answer was: —"It was never before heard that any good subjects did dispute the king's power in this point. What is it to you whether I make many or few boroughs? My council may consider the fitness if I require it : but what if I had created forty noblemen and four hundred boroughs? The more the merrier, the fewer, the better cheer."

Mathematicians (says Rabelais) allow the same horoscope to princes and to fools; and, however irreverent the notion may be, there are times when one is inclined to think the mathematicians right.

The impatience naturally felt by the adherents of the ROCK family at the unusual tranquillity which prevailed during this period, has been well expressed by one of my ancestors, in a spirited Irish ode, of which I have ventured to translate the opening stanzas, though without the least hope of being able to give any adequate idea of the abrupt and bursting energy of the original.

"RUPES sonant carmina."—VIRGIL.

Where art thou, Genius of Riot?
Where is thy yell of defiance?
Why are the Sheas and O'Shaughnessies quiet?
And whither have fled the O'Rourkes and O'Briens?

Up from thy slumber, O'Branigan!
Rouse the Mac Shanes and O'Haggarties!

[1] Strafford, too, in the following reign, seems to have made an equally unceremonious stride towards parliamentary influence :—"I shall labour," he says, in one of his letters, "to make as many captains and officers burgesses in this parliament as I possibly can; who, having immediate dependence upon the crown, may almost sway the business between the two parties which way they please."

Courage, Sir Corney O'Toole!—be a man again—
Never let Heffernan say " what a braggart 'tis!

Oh! when rebellion's so feasible,
    Where is the kern would be slinking off?
Con of the battles! what makes you so peaceable?
    Nial, the grand! what the dev'l are you thinking of?

CHAPTER VIII.

1625—1649.

Reign of Charles I.—Lord Strafford.—Perfect Despotism.—Hume's Notions of the " innocent and laudable."—Proposed Coalition between Captain Rock and the Emperor of Russia.—Fate of Strafford.

Lord Strafford was a man whom the lovers of arbitrary power ought to canonize; for seldom has more lustre been thrown over their bad cause than by "those rare abilities of his (as Lord Digby well expressed it), of which God gave him the use, but the devil the application."

His government in Ireland was, on a small scale, a perfect model of despotism [1], combining all the brute coercion of the East, with all the refined perfidy and Machiavelism of the West, and giving full rein to talents of the noblest breed, in the most unbounded career of oppression and injustice.

There are some of his acts which might almost turn men into rebels but to read; and yet Hume, to whom the severity of the Star-chamber appeared only " somewhat blameable," has, in the same spirit, styled the acts of Lord Strafford in Ireland, " innocent, and even laudable."

History has been called "philosophy teaching by examples "—and if the hearty concurrence of Strafford with the views of his perfidious master, in violating the solemn pledge given to the Catholics [2]—if his private advice to the monarch to disregard this pledge,

---

[1] In one of his letters he asserts triumphantly, " Now the king is as absolute here as any prince in the whole world can be."

[2] His promise to them of certain Graces or concessions, in return for those voluntary contributions with which they had assisted him in his necessities. The favours which they required of him (says Macdiarmid) "were certainly moderate. They related to certain abuses arising from a defective police; to exactions in the court of justice; depredations committed by the soldiery; monopolies which tended to the ruin of trade; penal statutes on account of religion; retrospective inquiries into defective titles," etc. etc.

Such were the evils, for the suppression of which these wretched people were obliged to bribe their monarch; and such was the monarch who could not only consent to sell justice to his people, but who could take the money first, and defraud them of the justice afterwards.

while he publicly rebuked the parliament for harbouring the least doubt of its sincerity [1]—if his readiness, when even Charles shrunk from the responsibility of such deceit, to take all the infamy of this transaction on himself [2]—if that unparalleled system of robbery, under the pretext of an Inquiry into Titles, to which, adopted with improved machinery from the preceding reign, he gave all the impulse of his powerful mind, and by which the whole province of Connaught became the booty of the crown and its minions—if the arbitrary measures by which he enforced this scheme of plunder, fining, pillorying, and branding such jurors as hesitated to find a title in the king—if his flagitious trial of Lord Mountnorris [3], where himself, the accuser, presided, and the only witness against the accused sat among the judges—if such transactions as these are to be held up as examples of the *innocent* and the *laudable,* then let Hume's own ‘‘Sceptic’’ take the world into his hands, and remove all those landmarks of right and wrong, of justice and injustice, by which honest men have hitherto steered; let tyranny and turbulence, perfidy and plunder, be the order of the day among rulers and their subjects; and let Captain Rock and the Czar of Russia divide the world between them. I shall not complain of *my* share in the arrangement, and I will answer for the magnanimous Alexander being equally satisfied with his.

[1] ‘‘ Surely,’’ he said, ‘‘ so great a meanness cannot enter your hearts as once to suspect his majesty's gracious regards of you, and performance with you, where you affix yourselves upon his grace.’’

[2] Charles thus acknowledges this faithful service of his ‘‘ *âme damnée :* ’’

‘‘ Wentworth,

‘‘ Before I answer any of your particular letters to me, I must tell you that your last public despatch has given me a great deal of contentment; and especially for the keeping off the envy of a necessary negative from me of those unreasonable Graces that people expected from me.’’

The undisguised selfishness of Charles appears also on another occasion, where, in recommending to Strafford's attention some grants on the Irish establishment, which he was either to concede or refuse, as the good of the service required, he says, ‘‘ yet so, too, as I may have thanks howsoever; that if there be any thing to be denied, you may do it, not I.’’

[3] Strafford's contempt for the law, except as an instrument of power, breaks out continually and impatiently in his letters. He was short-sighted enough to look upon the opinion of the judges, with respect to Ship-money, as ‘‘ the greatest service which the profession had rendered in his time to the crown.’’ In one of his letters, too, from Ireland, he boasts of the complete control which he had gained over all the ministers of justice, who now, ‘‘ ministering wholly to uphold the sovereignty, carried a direct aspect upon the prerogative of his majesty, and squinted not aside upon the vulgar and vain opinions of the populace.’’—*Strafford's State Letters.*

It is to be regretted that Mr. Macdiarmid did not make more use of these spirited and highly-characteristic letters. A biographer of Lord Strafford should make him tell his own story.

It is not, however, Hume alone that has contributed to throw a
false light round the memory of Lord Strafford. His able biographer,
Macdiarmid, has also, perhaps unconsciously, given somewhat too
softened a tone to the "*umbrata atque aspera*[1]" of his picture;
and has had the forbearance to go through the detail of such insulting enormities, without suffering one true spark of indignation to
"kindle as he runs."

The splendid talents of Lord Strafford, and the imposing dignity
of his death, may well justify a feeling of sympathy in his fate; but
there would be no living in this world if there were not such examples, to hang up in the hall where Power holds his revel, and,
like those awful mementos in the banqueting-rooms of the Egyp-
tians, chasten his pride and check the exuberance of his riot.

CHAPTER IX.

1641.

Remarks on Rebellions.—Well got up in Ireland.—Journal kept by one
of my Ancestors in 1641.—Extracts from it.—Hume's Misrepresenta-
tions. —Protestant Ghosts, deposed to by a Protetant Bishop.

To an amateur of Rebellions, like myself, the contemplation of
even an *old* Irish one is as gratifying as the study of a real *cinque-
cento* to a connoisseur—the skill with which the Government has
always furnished the materials for the work, being only equalled by
the *con-spirito* style in which the people have always executed it.[2]

There is extant in our family a journal kept by one of my ancestors, during the early part of the great Rebellion of 1641, and,
though the good old gentleman who wrote it was bedridden at the
time, and therefore could not share in the pastime that was going
on, the intense interest which he took in the progress of the revolt,
and the alternation of his hopes and fears, according as the Government threw in more or less fuel to the flame, are expressed with a
degree of earnestness and *naïveté*, which may render the perusal
of a few extracts not altogether unpleasant.

These details are also curious, as giving us an insight into the
process by which great Rebellions have always been got up in Ireland. The same drama, a little modernized, was acted over again
in 1798; and the prompter's book and stage directions are still at

---

[1] Fresnoy.

[2] This manufacture of rebellions began very early in our history. In the reign
of Henry III. (Leland tells us) in many places where the English had obtained
settlements, the natives were *first driven into insurrections by their cruelty, and
then punished with double cruelty for their resistance.*

hand in. the archives of Dublin Castle, whenever an able Orange manager shall be found to preside over a renewal of the spectacle.

"*September* 29 , 1641.—Matters took well. Sir William Parsons[1] hath but lately declared, at a public entertainment[2], that within a twelvemonth, no Catholic shall be seen in Ireland—have despatched this speech to Ulster, where Sir Phelim O'Neal will turn it unto good account. Also, Sir John Clotworthy hath said in the House of Commons, that the conversion of the Papists of Ireland is only to be effected by a Bible in one hand and a sword in the other. This, with a little engrafting of other matter thereon, cannot fail, in time, to bring forth good fruit.—That gallant gentleman, Roger Moore, is busy in the North : those robberies committed on his noble ancestors, whereby himself is made a beggar, do sorely haunt him.

"*October* 3.—Informers, it is said, have been to the Castle, to represent the unusual and suspicious resort of persons to the house of Sir Phelim O'Neal; as also the secret journeys of the Lord Maguire, etc. etc. But there is no fear that the Lords Justices will attend to these forewarnings. Rebellion is a goose that layeth golden eggs, and they, at least, will not be the fools to kill it.[3]

"*October* 25.—There wanted a puff to the flame in the North, and it hath come as seasonably as we could have desired. Certain petitions have been, at public assizes and other public places, made known and read to many persons of quality, purporting that the extirpation of the Catholics is at hand[4], and that all who will not forthwith turn Protestants, shall be hanged up at their own doors.

----

[1] One of the two Lords Justices.

[2] The Beaf-steak club of that day, I presume.

[3] They who looked more nearly into the characters and principles of the Lords Justices, conceived, and not without reason, that they by no means wished to crush the rebellion in its beginnings, but were secretly desirous that the madness of the Irish might take its free course, so as to gratify their hopes of gain by new and extensive forfeitures."—LELAND.

[4] That this was no visionary alarm may be proved from a variety of testimonies. "It is evident," says Dr. Warner, "from the Lords Justices' letter to the Earl of Leicester, then Lord Lieutenant, that they hoped for *an extirpation, not of the mere Irish only, but of all the old English families also that were Roman Catholics.*" Among many statements in Carte to the same purport, I shall select the following :—"There is too much reason to think, that as the Lords Justices really wished the rebellion to spread, and more gentlemen of estates to be involved in it, that the forfeitures might be the greater, and a general plantation be carried on by a new set of English Protestants all over the kingdom, *to the ruin and expulsion of all the old English and natives that were Roman Catholics;* so, to promote what they wished, they gave out speeches upon occasions, insinuating such a design, and that in a short time there would not be a Roman Catholic left in the kingdom."

This news hath been like a match unto the mine. Sir Phelim O'Neal hath already seized upon the castles of Charlemont and Mountjoy —Tanderagee hath been surprized by O'Hanlon—Sir Con Magennis is in possession of Newry, and a bold dash hath been made into Fermanagh by Roger Maguire. Blood-letting, however, is, as yet, but rare.; nor hath any province except Ulster yet risen.

" 26.—Yesterday, their Catholic lordships of the pale, Lords Gormanstown, Netterville, Fitzwilliam, Howth, Kildare, Fingal, Dunsany, and Slane, went to the Council to express their abhorrence of the conspiracy that hath broken forth, and to demand arms for their own defence, and the annoyance of the enemy. But the Lords Justices did dismiss them with much coldness and evasion, [1] and with but scant supply of arms, whereat they are, as might be expected, sorely mortified. Most marvellously do these Lords Justices play into our hands ; and if they but prosper in putting these great nobles of the pale into desperation, we shall, in truth, have rare work of it !

" *November* 10.—All again looks downward, and there seemeth but small chance of a general rising this winter. His Majesty hath writ over to the Lords Justices that he will no longer deceive his loving subjects of Ireland, but that, in the Parliament forthwith to be assembled, the long desired Graces shall be propounded and confirmed. Blank tidings these for our gallants in the North. Roger Moore may now go whistle after his fair Leinster domains, and Sir Phelim must turn the old Tyrone helmet into a drinking-cup. Our only hope is in the Lords Justices.

" *November* 17.—The Lords Justices have prorogued the Parliament without suffering the promised Graces to be therein propounded, or even mentioned, whereby all chance of a redress of grievances is happily at an end, and we may now expect a right merry winter. The byrnes of Wicklow were up on the 12th, the twenty-four O'Farrels of Longfort have joined, and the Tooles and Cavanaghs of Caterlogh are stirring.

" *November* 18.—Tidings just come to hand, that on the night of the 13th ult. the English and Scotch of Carrickfergus did issue forth, and attack and murder, in the island Magee, [2] 3000 men,

---

[1] In the same manner the offers of the Catholic gentry in 1798, to raise regiments, etc. were coldly rejected; and Mr. Plunkett stated, from his own knowledge, in the House of Commons, last sessions, that though, during the whole of the rebellion, the Roman Catholics were most anxious to enter into the yeomanry corps of Dublin, the Protestants almost invariably refused them admittance. So rigidly, at that period, was Sir William Parsons's receipt for the mixing up of a good rebellion attended to.

[2] There has been some controversy about the date of this massacre, but the testimonies for fixing it early in November preponderate.

women, and children, all innocent persons, there being as yet no appearance of revolt in that quarter. If this doth not cause all Ireland to rise on the sudden; then is the blood of her Macs run dry, and her ancient O's become cyphers indeed.

"19.—Already hath the scabbard been put away, since the foul adventure of island Magee; and, at Lurgan and other places, repayment hath been taken, with heavy interest, for the treachery of that night. Sir Phelim is now blooded, and we shall not soon see the end on't.

"*December* 3.—The Lords Justices have taken back with much insult the few arms entrusted to the Lords of the Pale, and banished them from Dublin, whereby the disaffection of these great nobles is decided, and they are already, it is said, communing with Roger Moore.

"*December* 4.—Colonel Coote hath, in reward of his murderous carnage at Wicklow, been appointed governor of Dublin.

"*December* 8.—There is an order of both Houses of the English Parliament, dated November 30, directing the Lord Justices to "grant his Majesty's pardon to all those who within a convenient time shall return to their obedience." This might, as the saying goes, spoil sport; but that the Lords Justices are too keen on their scent of forfeitures, to suffer themselves to be turned therefrom by any such clemency; accordingly, no proclamation of this nature hath appeared, and matters go on right riotously still. [1]

"*December* 9.—Munster will soon be up, for the Lord President hath gone thither to tranquillize it. He hath already put to death four persons at Ballyowen, hanged six innocent labourers at Ballymurrin, and eight at Ballygalburt; [2] and when those loyal gentlemen, the Butlers of Kilveylaghlen and Ballynakill, with the Lord Dunboyne at their head, alarmed by the ill blood which this cruelty had produced, did come to offer their services in preserving the peace of the province, the Lord President told them, in his hasty furious way, that ' they were all rebels alike, that he would not trust one soul of them, but thought it more prudent to hang the best of them.' Whether these noble gentlemen will continue to be loyal after such speeches, remains to be seen.

[1] Charles seems to have been too late aware of the mistake which he had committed in breaking faith with the Irish. In his answer to a declaration of the English House of Commons, he tells them, that "if he had been obeyed in the Irish affairs before he went to Scotland, and *had been suffered to perform his engagements to his Irish subjects, there had been no rebellion.*"—*Relig. Sacr. Carolinæ quoted by Curry.*

[2] The skill with which the county of Wexford was roused from its tranquillity in 1798, by the seasonable application of burnings, half-hangings, etc. was a palpable but improved copy of this expedition of the Lord President of Munster.

"*December.*—At last the Lords and Gentlemen of the Pale have declared themselves, and now the whole nation hath risen in arms. [1] The seal which their Supreme Council hath framed to itself, wherewith to seal all credentials of office, beareth first the mark of a long cross, then, on the right side, a crown; on the left a harp, with a dove above, and a flaming heart below the cross, with, round about, this inscription : '*pro Deo, et Rege, et patriâ Hiberniâ unanimes !*'"

I need not, I trust, apologize for the length of these extracts — they contain the concentrated essence of Irish history.

The venerable journalist has recorded several other items of this valuable receipt for rebellion, which was used with such effect by the Lords Justices of that time, and by them transmitted to all succeeding practitioners. "Thus (he says) on the 22d of March Mr. Hugh M'Mahon was put to the rack in the Castle of Dublin, and on the day following, Sir John Read suffered the same. [2] M. Patrick Barnwell of Kilbrue, who was racked the other day, is now found out to be wholly innocent, [3] and many apologies have been thereupon made to the old gentleman."

[1] " The Lords Justices being at length forced by the King to make some show of treating with these confederate Catholics, sent a messenger to their Supreme Council sitting at Ross, offering a safe conduct to any whom they might depute to represent their grievances to the king's commissioners. In order, however, to defeat the pretended object, the safe conduct contained, among other insulting expressions, the words 'odious rebellion,' applied to the proceedings of the Confederates; in consequence of which, these Catholic noblemen and gentlemen sent back the messenger with a high-spirited answer, saying, ' that they were not, they thanked God, in that condition, as to sacrifice their loyalty to the malice of any; and that it would be a meanness beyond expression in them, who fought in the condition of loyal subjects, to come in the repute of rebels to set down their grievances. *We take God to witness,* added they, *that there are no limits set to the scorn and infamy that are cast upon us, and that we will be in the esteem of loyal subjects, or die to a man.*' "

[2] Another imitation—" Many of the common people, and some even in circumstances of life superior to that class, particularly in the city of Dublin, were scourged, picketed, or otherwise put to pain, to force a confession of concealed arms or plots."—*Gordon's History of the Rebellion of* 1798.

[3] Some of the mistakes of 1798 might rival this; for instance—" Mr. Wright of Clonmel was seized by Mr. T. Judkin Fitzgerald, and flagellated almost to death by receiving five hundred lashes, merely for having in his pocket a letter written in the French language, upon an indifferent subject."—PLOWDEN.

The trial and execution of Sir Edward Crosbie, now universally acknowledged to have been innocent, was one of those atrocities which it would be difficult in any times to parallel. " Protestant loyalists " (says Mr. Gordon, himself a Protestant clergyman), " who came to give testimony in favour of the accused were

By such means as these—and I have given but a faint notion of their atrocity—was the country lashed up into that paroxysm of "wild justice," which, to this day, is denominated an "odious and unnatural rebellion," and in which, the readers of Hume's history are taught to believe, the whole guilt and barbarity lay on the side of the Irish. [1]

That there was, in a conflict so long and so violent, the usual quantum of horrors, which bigotry on both sides is always sure to generate, cannot be denied; but how far those Depositions are worthy of belief, on which the heaviest charges of cruelty against the Catholics rest, may be judged from the following specimen of their rationality.

It was deposed, that the ghosts of the Protestants drowned by the rebels at Portadown Bridge were seen for a long time moving in various shapes upon the river, and Doctor Maxwell, Bishop of Kilmore (one of the most credible, perhaps, of all the deponents), enters into grave particulars about these ghosts in his depositions, and describes them as "sometimes having been seen, day and night, walking upon the river; sometimes brandishing their naked swords; sometimes singing psalms, and at other times shrieking in a most hideous and fearful manner."

We see by this, too, that Protestant bishops occasionally can rival even Catholic ones in their deglutition of the miraculous.

---

forcibly prevented by the military from entering the court. Roman Catholic prisoners were tortured by repeated floggings, to force them to give evidence against him, and appear to have been promised their lives upon no other condition than that of his conviction."—*History of the Rebellion of* 1798.

[1] Sir John Temple, upon whose authority Hume chiefly rests, was about as trust-worthy a narrator of the events of 1642 as Sir Richard Musgrave has been of those of 1798; and so well understood was the appetite of this latter gentleman for the marvellous, that it was the favourite pastime of some humorists in Dublin, at the time when he was collecting materials for his History, to impose gravely upon him as true the most monstrous fictions, which he as gravely transferred to his dull pages, and of which, no doubt, some future Hume will avail himself, for the old, but never obsolete task of blackening the character of the Irish.

There has lately appeared a short Treatise on the Rebellion of 1641, by Mr. Matthew Carey of Philadelphia, in which the evidences, adduced by Temple and others, of a general conspiracy of the Irish Catholics at that period, are sifted with a considerable degree of acuteness, and most satisfactorily proved to be futile and incredible.

CHAPTER X.

Cromwell in Ireland.—The Irish nearly exterminated.—Advantages of Despatch.—Cromwell, the Devil, and the Orangemen.—Parallel between the Soldiers of Joshua and the Corporation of Dublin.

THE ancient name of Ireland was Innisfail, or the Island of Destiny; and, if there had been added " of *evil* Destiny," the name would have been but too truly prophetic of her history. Walsingham, who, in Elizabeth's time, wished the whole island sunk in the sea, breathed a kinder wish for it than he, in the least degree, intended; and, either to have been moved farther off into the Atlantic —"procul a Jove, sed procul a fulmine"—or to be (like Rabelais' island Médamothi) *no where,* are the only two desirable alternatives that could be offered to us.

As if no possible change of circumstances could exempt this wretched people from suffering, after having been so vigorously persecuted and massacred under the Royal government, as rebels, they were now still more vigorously persecuted and massacred under the Parliamentary government, as royalists; and what with the Lords Justices on one side, and Cromwell and Ireton on the other, assisted by a pestilence, which was the least cruel enemy of the whole, they were at last reduced to a state very nearly realizing that long desired object of English policy—their extirpation. Little more, indeed, was left of the Catholic population than was barely sufficient to give life to the desolate region of Connaught, into which they were now driven like herds of cattle by Cromwell, under the menace of a proclamation, that "all of them who, after that time, should be found in any other part of the kingdom, man, woman, or child, might be killed by any body who saw or met them;"— while their estates, which, at that time, constituted at least nine-tenths of the landed property of the country, were divided among his officers and soldiers, and among those adventurers who had advanced money for the war [1].

[1] A survey being made of all Ireland for this purpose, the best land was rated only at 4s. an acre, and some only at a penny; and the soldiers drew lots in what part of the kingdom their portions should be assigned them. " No man," says Carte, " had so great shares as they who had been instruments to murder the king. What lands they were pleased to call *unprofitable* (which were thrown in gratis) they returned as such, let them be never so good and profitable."

Lord Antrim's estate (says the same author), consisting of 107,611 acres, was allotted to Sir J. Clotworthy (afterwards Lord Massareue) and a few others, in consideration of their adventures and pay, which did not in all exceed the sum of 7000l.

Such was *Cromwell's* way of settling the affairs of Ireland—and if a nation *is* to be ruined, this method is, perhaps, as good as any. It is, at least, more humane than the slow lingering process of exclusion, disappointment, and degradation, by which their hearts are worn out under more specious forms of tyranny : and that talent of despatch [1] which Molière attributes to one of his physicians, is no ordinary merit in a practitioner like Cromwell :—

" C'est un homme expéditif, expéditif, qui aime a dépêcher ses malades, et quand on a à mourir, cela se fait avec lui le plus vite du monde." A certain military Duke, who complains that Ireland is but half-conquered, would, no doubt, upon an emergency, try his hand in the same line of practice, and like that "stern hero," Mirmillo, in the Dispensary,

> " While others meanly take whole months to slay,
> Despatch the grateful patient in a day! "

Among other amiable enactments against the Catholics at this period, the price of five pounds was set on the head of a Romish priest—being exactly the same sum offered by the same legislators for the head of a wolf. The Athenians, we are told, encouraged the destruction of wolves by a similar reward (five drachmas); but it does not appear that these heathens bought up the heads of priests at the same rate—such zeal in the cause of religion being reserved for times of Christianity and Protestantism.

" The Devil," says Shakspeare, " can cite Scripture for his purpose;" and the soldiers of Cromwell being told by their leader [2], that " the Irish were to be treated as the Canaanites were by Joshua," most piously acted up to the model set before them; and, accordingly, " all the spoils of the cities and the cattle they took for a prey unto themselves, and every man they smote with the edge of the sword, until they had destroyed them; neither left they any to breathe."

[1] Ludlow tells us in his Memoirs, that, being on his march, an advanced party met two of the rebels; "one of whom," says he, "was killed by the guard before I came up; the other was saved, and being brought before me, I asked him if he had a mind to be hanged? and he only answered, 'If you please.' So insensibly stupid (adds he) were many of these poor creatures."

Ludlow was mistaken—there was no stupidity here. Both the history and character of the Irish—their familiarity with the " plurima mortis imago ," and their careless contempt for it—were all expressed in the answer of this rebel.

[2] Cromwell's pious account of the surrender of Drogheda (where, having been admitted, on promise of quarter, he began a slaughter of the garrison which lasted five days) is a precious sample of this perversion of religion. "I wish," he says, in concluding his letter to the parliament, "that all honest hearts may give the glory of this to God alone, to whom indeed the praise of *this mercy* belongs."—WHITELOCKE.

A similar taste for the warlike passages of the Old Testament is observable in our modern Oliverians, Sir Abraham Bradley King, and his brother Orangemen; and, by a remarkable coincidence, it is from the same book, Joshua, that they, too, draw their charitable inspirations. How far these Orange heroes mean to carry their imitation of the soldiers of Joshua remains to be seen; but, I presume, the great victory which their leader Sir Abraham lately gained over the law by means of the House of Commons, was meant as a copy of the conquest of Jericho through the treachery of the harlot, Rahab—the House of Commons enacting the part of Rahab on the occasion.

Then, the ceremony of "taking twelve men out of the tribes" is as evidently followed in the selection of twelve good and true Orangemen for all purposes of impartial law and justice—and "the accused thing" which got among the soldiers of Joshua (meaning neither more nor less than a spirit of jobbing), has been long supposed to lie lurking among these faithfully scriptural Orangemen. "They have even taken of the accursed thing, and have also *stolen* and dissembled also, and *they have put it even among their own stuff.*"

When to these striking points of similitude, we add the perfect truth with which the whole body may say— "For even all the inhabitants of the country do faint because of us," it will be granted that in the art of "citing Scripture to their purpose," neither Cromwell nor the other personage mentioned by Shakspeare can, in any degree, compare with their modern imitators, the Orangemen.

CHAPTER XI.

1660—1684.

Reign of Charles II.—Loyalty of the Irish a superfluous Luxury.— Cromwell, Ireton, etc. declared loyal Protestant Subjects.—Their Followers rewarded.—Catholic Loyalists ruined.—Satirical Fictions.—Unsuccessful Attempt to get up a Rebellion in Ireland.—Only one Catholic Primate hanged.

" LOYALTY," Swift says, "is the foible of the Irish"—and it is certain that, whenever an opportunity has been allowed them, they have indulged in this " graceful weakness," even more than was either dignified or necessary. As it has been always, however, their fate to be equally ill-treated when loyal as when rebellious, their loyalty, except as matter of needless luxury to themselves, makes no difference in the relations between them and their rulers whatever.

The Catholics were the last in the three kingdoms to lay down the Royal banner, after suffering all but utter extermination in its defence. Yet, how was their devotedness rewarded at the Restoration? In one of the very first Acts that issued from the Royal hand—in order to furnish a pretext for confirming all the robberies of Cromwell—it was coolly and unblushingly declared that they were rebels [1]; and that, having been conquered by his Majesty's Protestant subjects (meaning Cromwell, Ireton, Lord Broghill, etc.), their estates and possessions became vested in the crown. This point once established, the path of iniquity lay clear and open; and upon such monstrous and insulting falsehoods was that Act of Settlement founded; "by which," says Lord Clare, "seven millions eight hundred thousand acres of land were set out to a motley crew of English adventurers, civil and military, nearly to the total exclusion of the old inhabitants of the island [2]."

If such things were read in Gulliver, Candide, or any such satirical fiction, they would be regarded as caricatures, too extravagant and distorted, of the perfidy and injustice of Kings and Governments. But when we not only know that such proceedings once took place, but see actual, existing men, who still cling to the *principle* of those proceedings, and dignify it with the name of "the wisdom of our ancestors," we feel that no romance can do justice to such perverse absurdity; and that Klemius, [3] who represents a man as ready to swear that the sun is triangular, in order to qualify for a place which requires that particular belief, would feel ashamed of the tameness of his satire, if he could but know how some of our statesmen transcend it.

It was, indeed, among the authors and patrons of this memorable Act of Spoliation that the idea of excluding Catholics from the House of Commons (one of the boasted proofs of the "wisdom of our ancestors") first originated. As Catholics were to be the persons despoiled, their concurrence could hardly be expected; and though the House was of Cromwell's own packing, and almost entirely composed of those soldiers and adventurers, who were to become, by this measure, the proprietors of near three-fourths of Ireland,

[1] These "rebels," when they were conquered, fought under the command of the Marquis of Ormond, his Majesty's Lord Lieutenant of Ireland, and of Lord Clanrickard, who was Deputy after him.

[2] "And thus," adds Lord Clare, "a new colony of new settlers, composed of all the various sects which then infested England, Independents, Anabaptists, Seceders, Brownists, Socinians, Millenarians, and dissenters of every description, many of them infected with the leaven of democracy, poured into Ireland, and were put into possession of the ancient inheritance of its inhabitants."—*Speech on the Union.*

[3] Journey under Ground.

4

yet, unwilling that Catholics should have a share even in their debates, they endeavoured to exclude them altogether from the
House, by rendering the Oath of Supremacy an indispensable qualification for a seat in it. The attempt, however, was resisted, at
the time, as an invasion of the prerogative; and the few Catholics
who were members had the melancholy privilege of witnessing the
formal transfer of so large a portion of their country to men, "who,"
as Swift says, "gained by rebellion what they and their fellow-
countrymen lost by loyalty [1]."

It may be perceived that, in remarking on the transactions of
this and other reigns, I seem for the moment to lose sight of my
own personal interest, and to kindle into serious indignation against
measures, on which the renown and prosperity of my family are
founded. But, whether it be that, like the man in Xenophon, I
have two souls—a soul for right, and a soul for riot—or that, in
such cases, I speak as a mere citizen of the world, certain it is
that I am not the less grateful to the " wisdom of our ancestors,"
for that inexhaustible Fund of Discord which it has bequeathed to
me and my family; nor a whit the less alive to the merits of those
personages of our own times, whether Chief Secretaries, lord
Chancellors, Aldermen, or Archbishops, who contribute weekly,
monthly, and annually their quotas to this venerable Fund, and
promise to make it as large and lasting a blessing as the Debt of
England itself.

There is one singularity in this reign, which well deserves to be
recorded—the English Ministry tried to get up a rebellion in Ireland, and could not!

When that chef-d'œuvre of bigotry and absurdity, the Popish
Plot (whose madness has left its slaver upon the policy of England
ever since), was at the full height of its fraud and frenzy, it was
thought, with justice, to be a reflection on the authenticity of the
conspiracy, that Ireland did not lend it the ready sanction of her
experience; and, accordingly, in addition to the usual provoca-
tions [2] of Penal laws, menaces of extermination, etc. etc., emissa-

---

[1] When the memorials of the Catholics, in justification of their claims, were
discussed before the English Council, the Commissioners from the Irish parliament
who attended upon this occasion, however they differed (says Lord Clarendon)
about their private interests, all agreed in their implacable malice to the Irish;
" insomuch that they concurred in their desire that they might gain nothing by
the King's return, but be kept with the same rigour and the same incapacity to
do hurt, which they were then under. And though eradication was too foul a
word to be uttered in the hearing of a Christian Prince, yet it was little less or
better, that they proposed, in other words, and hoped to obtain."—*Clarendon's
Life.*

[2] " There were too many Protestants then in Ireland," says Carte, " who

ries were despatched throughout the country in search of informers and witnesses, and the example of the pensioned Oates held out, to tempt villains of every creed and class into the same path of prosperity.

But all would not do. The Irish like their plots to be of home manufacture, and extend their hatred of imports even to that favourite article, rebellion—so much so, that when discontent is most abundant in England (as on the recent occasion of the Queen's trial) scarce a sample of it is to be seen in the Irish market.

The Duke of Ormond, too, who was Lord Lieutenant at this period, took a different method of keeping the peace from those which have been generally adopted since [1]. The Test Act, and the Bill for the expulsion of Popish Peers from Parliament, were among the scourges by which Shaftesbury and his party meant to lash up the people into revolt. But the Duke of Ormond by his influence prevented these measures from passing—being against them, as he expressed it, " in conscience, as well as in prudence; because he knew no reason why opinion should take away a man's birthright."

The only victim that the Protestant agitators could lay their hands upon to indemnify them for their trouble, was the Roman Catholic Primate of Ireland, Plunkett—" a wise and sober man," says Burnet, " fond of living quietly, and in due subjection to the Government, without engaging in intrigues of state." This, however, made no difference to his orthodox persecutors—he was hurried over to England, and condemned and executed at Tyburn, on the accusation of suborned witnesses, " who (again to use the language of Burnet) hearing that England was then disposed to hearken to good swearers, thought themselves well qualified for the employment."

wanted another rebellion, that they might increase their estates by new forfeitures. And letters were *perpetually sending into England misrepresenting the Lord Lieutenant's conduct,* and the state of things in England."

So like is one part of the history of Ireland to another, that in reading it, we are somewhat in the situation of that absent man, to whom D'Argenson lent the same volume of a work four successive times, and who, when asked how he liked the author, answered: " Il me semble qu'il se répète quelquefois." The Government of Ireland " se répète" with a vengeance!

[1] He was urged to imprison all the principal Roman Catholics of Ireland at this juncture, but he refused to do so. " It was well known," adds Leland, " how much the imprisonments and other severities of Sir W. Parsons had contributed to hurry numbers into the last rebellion; and neither the Duke nor the Privy Council deemed it prudent to make a similar experiment."

For this moderation and wisdom Ormond was, of course, hated and calumniated by the Protestant Ascendency of that day, and the same honourable tribute (as Lord Wellesley well knows) awaits every Lord Lieutenant who deviates into the same liberal course.

CHAPTER XII.

1685—1701.

Reigns of James II. and William III.—Irish Anomalies.—English Injustice.—Battle of the Boyne.—Forfeitures.—Vindication of William from the Orangemen.—The " glorious memory" of Titus Oates proposed instead.—Judge Scroggs's Wig.—Rapparees.—Relatives of the Rock Family.

Among the many anomalous situations in which the Irish have been placed by those " marriage vows, false as dicers' oaths," which bind their country to England, the dilemma in which they found themselves at the Revolution was not the least perplexing or cruel [1]. If they were loyal to the King *de jure*, they were hanged by the King *de facto*; and, if they escaped with life from the King *de facto*, it was but to be plundered and proscribed by the King *de jure* afterwards.

> Hac *gener* atque *socer* coeant mercede suorum.—Virgil.

> " In a manner so summary, prompt, and high-mettled,
> 'Twixt father and son-in-law matters were settled.''

In fact, most of the outlawries in Ireland were for treason committed the very day on which the Prince and Princess of Orange accepted the crown in the Banqueting-house; though the news of this event could not possibly have reached the other side of the channel on the same day, and the Lord Lieutenant of king James, with an army to enforce obedience, was at that time in actual possession of the government. So little was common sense consulted, or the mere decency of forms observed by that rapacious spirit, which nothing less than the confiscation of the whole island could satisfy; and which having, in the reign of James I. and at the Restoration, despoiled the natives of no less than ten millions six hundred and thirty-six thousand, eight hundred and thirty-seven acres, now added to its plunder one million, sixty thousand, seven hundred and ninety-two acres more, being the amount, altogther (according to Lord Clare's calculation), of the whole superficial contents of the island!

Thus not only had *all* Ireland suffered confiscation in the course

---

[1] Among the persons most puzzled and perplexed by the two opposite Royal claims on their allegiance were the clergymen of the Established Church; who, having first prayed for King James as their lawful sovereign, as soon as William was proclaimed took to praying for *him*; but again, on the success of the Jacobite forces in the north, very prudently prayed for King James once more, till the arrival of Schomberg, when, as far as his quarters reached, they returned to praying for King William again.

of this century, but no inconsiderable portion of it had been twice and even thrice confiscated. Well might Lord Clare say, "that the situation of the Irish nation, at the Revolution, stands unparalleled in the history of the inhabited world [1]."

Yet this is the period which our Orangemen have the face to celebrate!—and the day, which brought such ruin upon Ireland, is to be marked for ever among the Fasti of her Calendar, instead of being, if possible, erased from recollection for ever, as the fatal day of Pharsalia was by the Romans, beyond the power even of chronology to ascertain its date :—

> " Tempora siguavit leviorum Roma malorum,
> *Hunc voluit nescire diem.*"—LUCAN.
>
> Of all her days of sorrow, this alone
> Was left by Rome, even to herself unknown.

James was not fitted by nature for either of the tasks which he undertook,—neither for reducing a free people to slavery, nor for raising an enslaved race to freedom. He was in his true element at St. Germain, touching for the King's evil, and endeavouring in vain to make good Catholics of the Calvinist grenadiers and dragoons that had deserted to him [2].

Under such a leader, the ill-fated Irish, encumbered and distracted by English feuds, and strong only in hate, had but little chance against a people proud in the new exercise of their sovereign will, and under a chief so brave and so self-possessed as William. It was one of my ancestors (a Corporal ROCK of the brave Sarsfield's regiment), who, after the battle of the Boyne, spoke those well-known words, so pregnant with the feelings of mortified bravery, and so fully doing justice to both leaders,—"Change kings, and we'll fight it over again with you [3]!"

Unequal as was the conflict that ensued, the Irish, when disburdened of their king, fought it out manfully, and, had the common faith kept with enemies been observed towards them, would have

---

[1] "And if" (he as truly adds) " the wars of England, carried on here from the reign of Elizabeth, had been waged against a foreign enemy, the inhabitants would have retained their possessions under the established laws of civilized nations."—*Speech on the Union.*

[2] Prefixed to Count Hamilton's Zéneyde there is a description of the court of St. Germain, at once melancholy and diverting. One of the groupes in this picture is " Un père jésuite, grand convertisseur, entre un grenadier et un dragon anglais, tous deux déserteurs, mais qui me parurent plus fidèles à Calvin qu'au prince d'Orange."

[3] It is said to be the same witty corporal that invented the celebrated toast, " To the little gentleman in velvet," meaning the mole that threw up the hill over which *Crop* (King William's horse) stumbled.

derived from the struggle no ordinary advantages; as the Articles of Limerick, solemnly ratified under the great seal of England, gua-- ranteed to the Catholics those two essential rights, liberty of con-- science and security of property. But,—as if every compact be-- tween England and Ireland were to be read, like witches' prayers, backwards,—those very articles, on the faith of which the whole nation finally submitted, were not only grossly violated in every particular, but followed up, without any further provocation from the Catholics, by a system of the most odious persecution that ever disgraced the bloody annals of bigotry.

The consummation of this iniquitous code was reserved for the subsequent reign, but its beginnings were prompt and rapid in the present; and the acts for disarming Papists, for banishing all the regular clergy out of the kingdom, for preventing their intermar-- riage with Protestants, etc., etc., show the spirit in which the articles of Limerick were acted upon, even during the lifetime of him, who had pledged his royal honour to their fulfilment.

In justice, however, to William, as well as to the shame of those who still employ his name as a watch-word of persecution, it should never be forgotten that his own principles were completely adverse to the intolerant measures thus forced upon him. Before his expe-- dition to England, he wrote thus to the Emperor :—"I ought to entreat your Imperial Majesty to be assured, that I will employ all my credit to provide that the Roman Catholics of that country may enjoy liberty of conscience, and be put out of fear of being perse-- cuted on account of their religion."

His employment, too, of Irish Catholics in the army, was one of those criminal symptoms of a wish to make Papists useful and attached to the State, for which the English House of Commons rebuked him in their address of 1692; and there is but little doubt, that, could he have pursued his own liberal views [1], the same spirit that dictated his instructions to the commissioners of Scotland— "you are to pass an Act establishing that Church Government, which is most agreeable to the inclinations of the people"—would have also regulated his policy towards Ireland.

Even fettered and obstructed as he was by the bigotry of those about him, it is well known that, previously to the surrender of Limerick, he was prepared to offer to the Catholics no less advanta-

---

[1] Dryden thus, in one of his letters, does justice to the real disposition of William :—"We poor Catholics daily expect a most severe Proclamation to come out against us (the Five Mile Act), and at the same time we are satisfied that the King is very unwilling to persecute us, considering us to be but a handful, and those disarmed; but the Archbishop of Canterbury (Tennison) is our heavy enemy, and heavy he is, indeed, in all respects."—*Letters to Mrs. Stewart*, 1698 9.

geous terms ', than the free exercise of their religion, half the Church establishment of Ireland, and the moiety of their ancient properties!

What a heterodox idol, then, have the Orangemen set up unto themselves!—That pious and innocent Spaniard, who placed the picture of Lais in his oratory, and daily prayed to the fair Liberal as a Saint, was not more mistaken in the object of his idolatry than they are.

In the name of history, then, *why* do they not select some fitter Patron? That learned antiquary, Vallancy, has discovered, that the name, Patrick, which we Irish give to our National Saint, means the Devil : and the same sort of blunder seems to have been committed by the Orangemen, in the selection of *their* National Saint, King William—for who but the Devil would have offered half the Church Establishment to the Papists?

They must, therefore, lose no time in adopting some more appropriate Patron, and I would venture to recommended Titus Oates to their notice, as a Deliverer entirely after their own hearts. I would, myself (being anxious for the maintenance of their Institution, and regarding it as one of the main props of the ROCK dynasty) subscribe to a statue of old Titus for their use, which they might annually adorn and dress out with Judge Scroggs's wig—if it be still extant—and thus, by this double homage to the Informer and Judge, do justice to their own notions both of Civil and Religious Freedom. Lord Farnham will, I trust, attend to this friendly suggestion.

It was a little before the period of the Revolution, that an important branch of my family first rose into notice, under the name of *Rapparees*, or *Tories*—but as a full account of these heroes has been given in an interesting work called "the History of the Irish Rogues and Rapparees," it is unnecessary for me here to enter into any particulars about them, except just to remark, that one of their appellations, *Tories*, has been since transferred to an equally valuable class of his Majesty's subjects, who have done as much mischief, at the head of affairs, as the others have at the tail, and who, though in no way related to me, have served me on all occasions even more effectually than if they were.

' This was called (says Leland) the "Secret Proclamation," because, though printed, it was never published, having been suppressed on the first intelligence of the Treaty of Limerick.

CHAPTER XIII.

1701—1727.

Reigns of Anne and George I.—Fate of Pope, if born in Munster.—
Penal Code.—Swift.—His Notions of Tolerance.—Wood's Halfpence.
—Independence of Ireland.—Barbarous Law against Romish Priests.
—Hints for putting down the Rock Family.

In the reign of Queen Anne, the degradation and enslavement of the great mass of the Irish nation was completed; and at a time when a Catholic poet was illuminating the literature of England, with that true light of genius which never dies, in Ireland to be a Catholic was to be an outcast from the commonest privileges of humanity;—so that, if Pope had been born a Munster Papist, instead of a London one, by Act 7 William and Mary, and 2 Anne, he would have been voted an irreclaimable brute, and hunted into the mountains.

The Penal Code, enacted at this period, will for ever remain a monument of the atrocious perfection, to which the art of torturing his fellow-creatures may be brought by civilized man. It was truly, as Burke calls it, "a machine of wise and elaborate contrivance, and as well fitted for the oppression, impoverishment, and degradation of a people, and the debasement in them of human nature itself, as ever proceeded from the perverted ingenuity of man."

There was more blood drawn by Dioclesian, and other heathen bunglers in persecution; but the refinement of wasting away the hearts of a whole people by piecemeal was reserved for the Christian and Protestant legislators of Queen Anne. Let us not, however, give all our execrations to *them,* and their now half broken-up machinery of oppression—let us keep some for those persons (and they are neither few nor obscure) who at this moment still sigh after those good old penal times—who consider liberality and justice as degeneracy from their ancestors, and who try to infuse into every remaining fragment of that polypus of persecution, the same pestilent life that pervaded the whole.

With this part of his country's history, an Irish Chronicler has little else to do than to mourn over it and be silent.—The chief actors in the scene can hardly be called Irishmen, and the sufferers in the back-ground were all mute and nameless.

The best and most patriotic men of the time were but (as Swift styles Molyneux, and, by implication, himself) "Englishmen born here." Swift's own patriotism was little more than a graft of English faction upon an Irish stock—fructifying, it is true, into such splendid produce, as makes us proud to think it indigenous to the soil. How little his views of toleration expanded beyond the circumference of those about him, appears from the violence with which he always opposed the claims of the Dissenters; and for the misery and degradation of his Roman Catholic countrymen (who constituted, even then, four-fifths of the population of Ireland), he seems to have cared little more than his own Gulliver would for the sufferings of so many disfranchised Yahoos.

The following passage not only proves the inoffensiveness of this race of victims at that time [1], but is a specimen of the truly Spartan *sang-froid*, with which even the Patriot Swift could contemplate such a system of Helotism. "We look upon them," he says, "to be altogether as inconsiderable as the women and children. Their lands are almost entirely taken from them, and they are rendered incapable of purchasing any more; and for the little that remains, provision is made by the late act against Popery, that it will daily crumble away. In the mean time, the common people, without leaders, without discipline, or natural courage, being little better than hewers of wood and drawers of water, are out of all capacity of doing any mischief, if they were ever so well inclined."

The affair of Wood's halfpence, upon which so much of Swift's wit was lavished—"*ære ciere viros*"—though magnified at the time into more than its due importance, is interesting even now, as having been the first national cause, round which the people of

---

[1] His Pamphlet, also, entitled "Reasons for repealing the Test in favour of the Roman Catholics," in which he ironically brings forward the claims of the Catholics, as far superior to those of the Dissenters, abundantly proves to what a hopeless state the former class were reduced, when the very justice of their cause could be sported with so safely, and the strongest reasons for their enfranchisement adduced as a sort of *argumentum ad absurdum*, under the perfect security that such a result was impossible.

Sometimes, indeed, his good sense, as well as his hatred to the Whigs, led him to laugh at the prevalent alarms about Popery; and, in one instance, the circumstances to which he alludes show to what ludicrous lengths the Ascendency Spirit was at that time carried. In the Journals of the Irish House of Commons, there is a Petition presented by the Protestant porters of Dublin against one Darby Ryan, "a Captain under the late King James, and a Papist notoriously disaffected, who bought up whole cargoes of coals, and employed those of his own persuasion and affection to carry the same to customers, by which the petitioners were debarred and hindered from their small trade and gains."

On another occasion it appears from the Journals that the Hackney Coachmen of Dublin asserted the Ascendency of the Box with a similar spirit, and prayed the House *that it might be enacted that none but Protestant hackney-coachmen might have liberty to keep and drive hackney-coaches,* etc. etc.

To these circumstances Swift is supposed to allude, when, with his usual happy humour, he remarks that, if the Dublin Cries are allowed to continue, "they ought to be only trusted in the hands of Protestants, who had given security to the Government."

Ireland had ever been induced to rally. What neither Christian charity nor the dictates of sound policy could effect, an influx of brass
halfpence brought about at once, and Protestant, Catholic, and
Presbyterian, uniting for the first time, opposed themselves to their
English governors, and triumphed over them and their halfpence.

The danger of such a union, momentary and unimportant as it
was, to the precious Palladium of the Protestant Interest, did not
escape the observation of those who, as usual, founded that interest on the eternal division and disunion of the people. Accordingly
we find Primate Boulter complaining thus in a letter to the duke of
Newcastle : " I find that the people of every religion, country, and
party here, are alike set against Wood's halfpence, and that their
agreement in this *has had a most unhappy influence on the state
of this nation, by bringing on intimacies between Papists and
the Whigs, who before had no correspondence with them.*"

This war against Wood's halfpence is also remarkable, for having
incidentally brought into discussion that once animating, but now
extinguished, question of the Independence of Ireland, and it shows
how the higher Spirits of this world, like those of the world above
us, " cry out one unto another," through the waste of time; for,
the same principles which Swift asserted at this period, were echoed
by Grattan at the glorious era of 1782, when the dream of both patriots was for a short moment realised.

Among the many freaks of wanton and exuberant cruelty in
which the legislators of these two reigns luxuriated, there was one
measure respecting Popish priests, which I know not how to describe except by saying that it deserves, perhaps, *par excellence,*
the designation of a *Penal* Law, and by referring for the atrocious
particulars to Curry, Plowden, and other historians. This proposition, it is said, was not only heard, but acceded to, by the Irish
House of Commons, and transmitted, with the particular recommendation of the Lord Lieutenant, to England. But the Cabinet
there, not quite so far gone in barbarism, rejected it with indignation.

So low in the scale of humanity may men be reduced by that
false spirit of religion,

> " Which boasts from heaven the sacred spell,
>   But reads it by a light from hell!¹ "

If I am asked what became of my ancestors during this still and
stagnant interval, I feel somewhat at a loss how to answer—being
aware that in acknowledging them to have been as quiet and well-
behaved, as an American bear in his winter quarters, I give a

¹ Curran.

triumph to those sages, both of Church and State, who consider Penal laws to be the only true sedatives of the ROCK spirit.

But I will even go farther, and grant that the Penal system, as then organized, *was* most eminently calculated to ensure tranquillity; and that a people in the state described by Swift, must have been as tame and harmless as the petrified population of that City described in the fables of the East.

There are but two ways, in short, of keeping down the ROCK family; either by restoring the Penal code to its full, original perfection, or by abolishing, in spirit as well as in deed, all the odious remains of it. The former of these modes our rulers *cannot* adopt, and the latter, I know, they *will not.* Thus secured by the strength of the people from *one* remedy, and guaranteed by the eternal folly of our Government against the *other,* what have I to fear for the permanence and prosperity of our race ? May I not rather hope, that, like our namesakes, the *Romans,* we shall be hailed throughout all time,

Romanos, rerum dominos, *gensemque togatam.*
Law, peace, and justice, at our feet shall fall,
And *the white-shirted* ' *race* be lords o'er all!

CHAPTER XIV.

1727—1760.

Reign of George II.—An Event of much Importance to the Rock Family. —The Clergy among our best Friends.—Abolition of the Agistment Tithe.—Its Consequences.—Conclusion of the First Book.

IN the eighth year of the reign of George II., some twenty-seven years before I was born, an event happened whose consequences have been so important to me and my family, that it deserves a more than ordinary notice in this Sketch.

Of all the purveyors of grievances to whom The ROCKS have been indebted, the Clergy, it must be owned, have not been the most backward—but have gone on regularly supplying us with that raw material of discontent, which we know so well how to manufacture to our own taste afterwards. They began these services to us immediately at the Reformation, as appears from Spencer's description of the Protestant clergy of that time. " Besides these vices (he says after running through some trifling items of ' gross simony, greedy covetousness, fleshly incontinence,' etc. etc.) they have particular

---

' The costume adopted by the White-boys, Shanavests, and other Rock associations.

enormities. They neither read the Scriptures, nor preach to the people; only they take the tithes and offerings, and gather what fruits they can off their livings, which they convert as badly."

Of the Bishops of that period, too, the same author says : "They do not at all bestow the benefices which are in their own donation upon any (clergyman), but keep them in their own hand, and set their servants, or horse-boys, to take up the tithes and fruits of them."—Thus we see how worthy of the divine origin attributed to them, is the mode in which tithes have always been collected and managed in Ireland,—beginning with the "horse-boys" of the newly reformed Bishops, and ending with the drunken drivers and constables, employed in the service of the Church at present.

It cannot be doubted, that these Reverend gentlemen, and the ROCKS, must, from the first, have come frequently into collision with each other; but in the reign of George II., the Parliament interfered between them, and, with the usual object of such interpositions—to plunder both.

The Tithe of Agistment, the least objectionable of any, as falling upon that class of occupiers which could best afford to pay it, was, nevertheless, considered by these Honourable land proprietors (who were of Falstaff's opinion, that "base is the slave that pays,") a burthen not fit for gentlemen to bear. They accordingly abolished it '—at the same time, assuring the Clergy, whom they thus despoiled of their most profitable tithe, that it was all for the "Protestant Interest" they did so; and handing them over for their support to the "tillers of the land," and to those wretched cottiers—the very poorest of poverty's children—upon whom the burthen of the Protestant establishment has, ever since, principally lain.

The consequences of this Vote to me and my family, and the increased sphere of activity which it has opened to us, may be judged from the events of the last sixty years.

> " Inde (fide majus) *glebæ* cœpere moveri :
> .   .   .   crescitque *seges clypeata* virorum."—OVID.
>
> Then first the Men of Glebes awak'd to strife,
> And pike-arm'd *Crops* sprung every where to life.

I have thus given a faint and rapid sketch of the chief measures taken by our English masters, from the time of Henry II. to the

' For a full account of the proceedings on the Agistment Tithe at this period, see Mr. William Monck Mason's laborious and valuable *History of St. Patrick's Cathedral.* Mr. Mason's notices of the Life and Writings of Swift are full of new and interesting matter, and his enthusiasm for the memory of a great man (though sometimes carried a little too far) is highly honourable to his feelings as an Irishman.

accession of his late Majesty, to civilize and attach the Irish people.
I shall now proceed to show, in a brief review of my own times,
how steadily the same system has been pursued ever since, with the
same happy results to the government, to the people, and to me.

Matthew Lanesburgh—the Francis Moore of the continent—in
apologizing for the delay of his Almanack for 1824, pretty plainly
intimates that it was owing to the interference of the Holy Alliance,
who had denounced some parts of his works as dangerous to the
peace of Europe; "I have, therefore," he says, "consented to
sacrifice these passages, because, *je tiens infiniment à ce qu'on
me lise.*"

From the same motive I have, myself, in the course of these
pages, rejected many historical facts and documents, though of
considerable importance to the illustration of my subject; because I
am well aware that, in the present times, matter-of-fact has got
much into disrepute, and that statements, to be at all listened to,
must be measured by a minute-glass—because I know, too, that of
all the *bores* of the day, poor Ireland is (what some of her antiquarians wish to prove her) *Hyper*-borean—and because, in short,
like the worthy almanack-maker just mentioned, "*je tiens infiniment à ce qu'on me lise.*"

BOOK THE SECOND.

OF MY OWN TIMES.

Hic saltem monitis parere paternis.
(OVID.)

BOOK THE SECOND.

CHAPTER I.

Birth of Captain Rock.—Some Account of his Father.—Penal Laws.—
  Enactments with respect to Property.—Beggary of the Rock Family.—
  Levellers.—White-boys. - Christening of the Captain.—Brought up
  to the Tithe Line.—Remarkable Prophecy.

I WAS born in——, in the province of Munster, about the beginning of the year 1763. My father, though the head and represen-
tative of our ancient family, had been for a great part of his life as
quiet and suffering a Papist as the Protestant Ascendancy could, in
its most fastidious moments, require. Even the Scotch rebellion of
1745 appealed in vain to his hereditary sympathies ; nor could all
the pains taken by the government on that and other occasions, to
persuade him and his family that they were notorious rebels, produce any overt-act that at all resembled such a propensity.

One of the counsellors of the crown, in the year 1743, when
there was an alarm of a French invasion, went so far as to suggest,
that as the Papists one hundred years before had begun a massacre
on the Protestants, the Protestants ought now to return the compli-
ment, by falling in the same unceremonious manner upon the Papists. But even this hint was lost upon my imperturbable father.
Not only he, but four-fifths of his countrymen seemed sunk into
such a close resemblance of beasts of burthen, as might have gone
far to satisfy that doubter mentioned by Bolingbroke, who said " he
never could believe that slavery was of divine institution, till he
beheld subjects born with bunches on their backs like camels, and
kings with combs upon their heads like cocks." Whether the Papists
of that period had bunches on their backs, is not ascertained—but
that they were treated as if they had, is agreed on all sides.

An event, however, happened a few years before I came into the
world, which at length roused all the family spirit in my father,
and drove him to take that station in the affairs of Ireland, which
the House of ROCK seems destined, at all times, to assume.

5

As property and education are the best securities against discontent and violence, the Government, in its zeal for the advancement of our family, took especial care that we should be as little as possible encumbered with either. Of the quantity and quality of our education I shall speak in a subsequent chapter; but of the pains taken by our rulers to prevent us from being spoiled by property, some idea may be formed from a few of their enactments on the subject.

By the laws which existed when I was born, and for many years afterwards, Papists were declared to be incapable of purchasing estates, or of taking lands, farms, or houses, for a longer period than thirty-one years; and lest, under this short and precarious tenure, they might contrive to acquire a dangerous degree of competence, there was a clause in the Act obliging them to pay two-thirds of the profit-rent to the landlord, leaving them only the other third for the expense of tillage and subsistence. Upon any infraction of these provisions, either from the lenity of the landlord, or from any private arrangement between him and his tenant, the whole property so situated became the prey of the first Protestant discoverer, who was lucky enough to detect the transaction, and bring it before the courts of law.

If, notwithstanding these difficulties, a Roman Catholic contrived to secure a few gleanings from the scythe of the Law, any one of his sons (no matter how young—for Protestants of all sizes were thankfully received) might, by professing to become a convert to the Established Church, not only enter into immediate possession of a considerable part of his father's fortune, but constitute himself, by this act of conversion, heir-at-law to the whole, with full power to mortgage, sell, or otherwise alienate the reversion of it from his family for ever [1].

My father was one of those industrious Papists, who had managed to "deceive the Senate" and make themselves easy and comfortable. He had even purchased privately a small estate, which he was about

---

[1] In an address presented by the Catholics to the late king, in the year 1775, this grievance is thus stated :—" By the laws now in force in this kingdom, a son, however undutiful or profligate, shall not merely, by the merit of conforming to the established religion, deprive the Roman Catholic father of that free and full profession of his estate, that power to mortgage, or otherwise dispose of it, as the exigencies of his affairs may require; but shall himself have full liberty immediately to mortgage or otherwise alienate the reversion of that estate from his family for ever;—a regulation by which a father, contrary to the order of nature, is put under the power of his son, and through which an early dissoluteness is not only suffered but encouraged, by giving a pernicious privilege, the frequent use of which has broken the hearts of many deserving parents, and entailed poverty and despair on some of the most ancient and opulent families in this kingdom."

to transfer in trust to a poor Protestant barber, who had long made himself convenient to Roman Catholic gentlemen in this way [1], and who, though his own property did not exceed a few pounds in value, actually held in fee the estates of most of the Catholic gentry in the county. Let me add, too, for the honour of human nature and periwig-making, that, though the Legislature had set a high premium on perfidy, and even declared by a Resolution, which is to be seen on their journals, that "prosecuting and *informing against* Papists was an *honourable* service to the government, this Protestant barber was never known to betray his trust, but remained the faithful depositary of this proscribed wealth, which an "honourable" hint to the law officers would have made his own for ever.

Before, however, my father was able to effect the transfer, an informer had put the proper authorities in possession of the secret, and—I blush to state it—his informer was one of his own sons [2]; who, the day after he had thus betrayed his father, was received a welcome convert into the bosom of the Established Church.

This precious system of proselytism, which hoped to make good Protestants out of bad sons, and to improve the religion of the people by ruining their morals, succeeded but little with the obstinate Irish, who remained attached to their faith and their fathers in spite of it. My unlucky brother, indeed (or rather half-brother, for he was by the second Mrs. Rock, and I by the third), formed a sad exception to this honourable character; and was altogether a convert worthy of a Church, which could take such means to recruit its ranks. In his double capacity of informer and proselyte,

---

[1] Instances of this highly honourable humanity were not uncommon among the Protestants at that time. "Neither the menaces of power," says Mr. O'Connor, "nor the contagion of example, nor the influence of religious hatred, nor the prejudices of party, could eradicate the seeds of humanity. They connived at, encouraged, and aided evasions of the penalties and provisions of these iniquitous statutes. Many of them concealed proscribed priests in their houses, and became trustees or purchasers of properties and settlements of estates for Catholics, in order to favour their industry, and protect them from the ruin of the gavel act."— *History of the Irish Catholics.*

In order, however, to frustrate this humane interference, the spiteful Legislature brought in a bill, enacting that " all leases or purchases, in trust for Papists, shall belong to the first Protestant discoverer, and that no plea or demurrer should be allowed to any bill of discovery, relative to such trusts, etc. "

[2] I must say, for the honour of the family, that the mother of this unnatural young Rock was suspected of having some of the Cromwell blood in her veins, being descended, as it was whispered, from an Oliverian drummer ; whereas, the third Mrs. Rock was a regular O'Brien, counting back in a right line, through Aoife, the daughter of Dealbha, the son of Cas, the son of Conall-Eachluath, and so on up to the Munster knights of Tradaire, *ante Christum.*

he entered into possession of all the earnings of many a long day
of toil, and my father and the rest of the family were reduced to
beggary [1].

Let it always be recollected that the laws which encouraged such
crimes, were not the relics of any dark superstitious age, but
had been enacted in one of the golden periods of English literature,
and remained, like "phantoms, wandering by the light of day [2],"
amidst the general and increasing illumination of Europe.

Thus beggared, and, as it were, disinherited by his own child,
my father (the antiquity of whose ancestry was, as the reader has
seen, sufficiently venerable, to justify the mortification which he
felt at this reverse) was obliged, in the decline of life, to "join
the labouring train," and sink into that class of wretched colliers,
who then, as now, occupied the very Nadir of human existence.

It was not long before he felt the good effects of poverty and oppression, in quickening and bringing into play the hereditary ten-
dencies of his nature; but the first public occasion on which he
displayed his talents (though traceable, like all our other opportu-
nities of distinction, to the measures of the Government), was less
directly connected with Church and State than those which succeeded.

The origin of my father's *début* in Insurrection was as follows:—

The landlords of Munster, tempted by an increased demand for
pasturage, had inclosed those commons [3] on which they had given
their poor tenants a right of feeding; and either turned whole
swarms of those wretches out of their scanty holdings, or left them
at the mercy of greedy monopolists (at that time called "land-pi-
rates," but since honoured with the less offensive name of Middlemen), who, having bid an enormous rent for these newly-inclosed
lands, wrung a proportionate rent out of the miserable tenants to
whom they underlet them. Such was the first occasion, on which
my father's talents were brought into active service.

Though our family had been so little heard of for the last seventy
or eighty years, yet, in one respect, they had been by no means

[1] Mr. O'Connor, the learned Irish antiquary, used to relate, as his biographer
tells us, that his father, after the Revolution, was obliged to plough his own fields,
and that he would often say to his sons, "Boys, you must not be insolent to the
poor. I am the son of a gentleman, but ye are the children of a ploughman."

[2] Rogers's Columbus.

[3] In the reign of Edward VI. there were insurrections in England from the
same cause. "Whole domains" (says Mr. Southey) "were depopulated for the
purpose of converting them into sheep-farms. To such an extent was this inhuman
system carried, that a manifest decrease of population appeared in the muster-
books."—*Book of the Church.*

idle. They were, as Swift says, "the principal breeders of the nation;" and when to this enormous increase of their numbers, we
add the large stock of misery and ignorance which, under the auspices of the Government, they had been laying in all that time, it
must be granted that, on their re-appearance in public life, they
came eminently qualified to attract attention—and to take that lead
in the affairs of Ireland, which, under the same government patronage, they have maintained to the present day.

The first title which my father and his adherents assumed, was
that of Levellers—their interference with public matters being as
yet confined to levelling inclosures of commons, turning up new-
made roads, and other little *praeludia* of outrage and violence.
They were soon, however, summoned to a higher sphere of action.
The Tithe system began to attract my worthy father's attention [1],
and to disclose to him those inexhaustible sources of discord, which
have made it one of the best cards in the hands of our family ever
since.

As the Clergy found the sources of their incomes diminished by
the extension of pasturage, they pressed in proportion more heavily
on that indigent class of occupiers, whom the quantity of land
thrown out of tillage left chiefly chargeable with their support. To
be ground down by a hardhearted landlord was galling enough to
the poor Catholic; but to have both body and spirit wasted away in
thankless labour, in order to support in luxury the ministers of that
religion, by which his own faith was proscribed, his children
tempted to turn traitors, and himself chained down in misery and
bondage—this indeed was a refinement in misery,—a sort of com-
plicated infliction, which, if ever the art of driving a people mad
should again become the study of a Christian government, deserves
to be remembered among its most efficacious rules.

To reform this grievance was the object of my father's second appearance in the field, and his followers on that occasion took the
name of Whiteboys—a title adopted, as I have already explained,
on account of the white shirts they wore, and long the most favourite

---

[1] Attempts have been made to prove that Tithes were not considered a grievance
before this period—(See an *Inquiry*, etc. by J. N.), but the following observations
in an *Essay on the Trade of Ireland*, by Arthur Dobbs, Esq. published in 1729,
will show that they have been consistent in their obnoxiousness throughout—
indeed where, or when have Tithes *not* been considered a grievance?—" The
present method of setting, levying or recovering Tithes in this kingdom is frequently the ground of complaint, and an occasion of differences and coldness
between the Clergy and Laity in many places; which obstructs the Clergy's being
useful as spiritual guides, and has lately been made a handle to induce thousands
of the Protestant dissenters to go to America."

of all those " vagrant denominations, by which" (as Mr. Grattan says) " tumult delights to describe itself."

And here we have an instance of the truth of that memorable saying of Lord Redesdale—that " there is in Ireland one law for the rich, and another for the poor;"—a sentence which ought to be written up, like the "*Lasciate ogni speranza,*" over the door-way of every inferior Law court in Ireland.

In 1735, the land-owners had combined against the Agistment tithe,—had formed illegal associations in almost every county, to defray the expenses of resisting this claim, and indemnify those who had suffered by resisting it. But did the Legislature punish these gentlemen White-boys? On the contrary, they turned White-boys themselves; and, defying both judges and clergy, settled the matter as summarily as Captain Rock himself could have done.

In 1762, 1786, etc., etc., the miserable and starving cottiers, upon whom those Protestant land-holders had thrown the whole support of the Protestant church, dared to imitate their betters (in all but injustice), and combined against an exaction unparalleled in the annals of tyranny. It is needless to say what was the difference of their fate—transportation—hanging—acts " calculated for the meridian of Barbary [1];"—every thing but relief, compassion, or even inquiry.

It has been supposed that, in addition to his organization and command of the White-boys, my father also lent his powerful aid to the Oak-boys and Hearts-of-Steel; the former of whom took arms the following year, 1763, to get rid of a species of Corvée, called the six days labour, and the latter, some years afterwards, in consequence of various acts of oppression on the estate of an absentee

---

[1] Arthur Young, in speaking of the White-boys of this period, says:—" Acts were passed for their punishment, which seemed calculated for the meridian of Barbary; this arose to such a height, that by one they were to be hanged, under circumstances, without the formalities of a trial; which, though repealed the following sessions, marks the spirit of punishment : while others remain the law of the land, that would, if executed, tend more to raise than quell an insurrection. From all which it is manifest that the *gentlemen of Ireland never thought of a radical cure, from overlooking the real cause of disease , which in fact lay in themselves, and not in the wretches they doomed to the gallows. Let them change their own conduct entirely , and the poor will not long riot. Treat them like men who ought to be as free as yourselves. Put an end to that system of religious persecution which has for seventy years divided the kingdom against itself. In these two circumstances lies the cure of insurrection : perform them completely, and you will have an affectionate poor, instead of oppressed and discontented vassals.*"—Tour of Ireland.

Here is sound sense, spoken fifty years ago—and yet how little good it has done! Well may we say, with Congreve, " Who would die a martyr to sense, in a country where the religion is folly ?"

nobleman—like those by which the agent of Lord Courtenay lately drove the county of Limerick into revolt.

As the two latter insurrections were composed chiefly of Northern Protestants, some over strict Catholics have doubted whether my father would condescend to meddle with them. But the Rocks are no bigots in fighting matters; nor indeed at all particular as to whom they fight *with*, so it be but *against* the common enemy, —i. e. generally speaking, the Constituted Authorities for the time being. I can easily, therefore, believe that my venerable parent belonged not only to White-boys, Oak-boys, Heart-of-Steel boys, but to all other fraternities of Boys then existing, whose sports were at all likely to end in the attitude thus described by Virgil : — " Ludere *prudentes pueros.*"

In the midst of all these transactions I came into the world, — on the very day (as my mother has often mentioned to me, making a sign of the cross on her breast at the same time,) when Father Sheehy, the good parish priest of Clogheen, was hanged at Clonmell on the testimony of a perjured witness, for a crime of which he was innocent as the babe unborn. This execution of Father Sheehy was one of those *coups d'état* of the Irish authorities, which they used to perform at stated intervals, and which saved them the trouble of further atrocities for some time to come.

As Tithe matters seemed likely to occupy so much of the attention of our family, and I happened to be my father's tenth son, it struck him, that the ancient Irish Custom of dedicating the tenth child to the service of the Church, might be revived in my person with considerable propriety. He accordingly had me christened *Decimus* (which he had learning enough to know was Latin for " Tenth"), and resolved, if my talent lay that way, to bring me up exclusively to the Tithe department. How far my career in this sacred line has justified his fond paternal hopes, it is not for me to determine. I can only say, that it has always been my pride and ambition to uphold the glory of the name of ROCK, and transmit it with, if possible, increased lustre to my descendants.

I should mention also, among the motives that determined him to this step, a singular Prophecy, which had long existed in our family —and which, though little heeded by him in the time of his comfort and hope he now clung to with that fondness of belief of which a good Catholic, driven to despair, alone is capable. It ran thus :

> As long as Ireland shall pretend,
>   Like sugar-loaf turn'd upside down,
> To stand upon its smaller end,
>   So long shall live old ROCK's renown.

As long as Popish spade and scythe
Shall dig and cut the Sassanagh's [1] tithe;
And Popish purses pay the tolls,
On heaven's road, for Sassanagh souls—
As long as Millions shall kneel down
To ask of Thousands for their own,
While Thousands proudly turn away,
And to the Millions answer "nay"—
So long the merry reign shall be
Of Captain Rock and his Family.

CHAPTER II.

Attention of the Government to the education of the Rocks.—Institutions
for that purpose.—Charter Schools.—Royal Free Schools.—Some account of them.—Activity of the Church in the same laudable cause.—
Diocesan Schools.—Parochial Schools.—Present state of them.—Some
account of the different educating Societies.—Kildare Street, London
Hibernian, etc.

WE have seen with what care Government, during the last century, provided against any degeneracy in our family, by never let-
ting us rise, on the scale of property, higher than zero. Rockism,
indeed, like the *malaria*, only acts to a certain distance from the
ground,—those who stand erect, are in little danger from it, and
the prostrate alone take the infection properly. Guided by this experience, our rulers, landlords, clergy, etc. have co-operated success-
fully even to the present day in keeping down the great mass of the
people to that exact pitch of depression, at which the contagion of
Rockism is always found to be most malignant.

With such skilful provisions on the subject of Property [2], as I

[1] The Irish term for a Protestant, or Englishman.

[2] In the Second Report of the Deputation sent by the Draper's Company of
London, to visit their estates in the County of Londonderry, in the years 1817
and 1818, there are the following sensible and liberal remarks on this subject:
—Observing upon the great proportion of poor individuals belonging to the Roman
Catholic church, the Reporters say:—" This circumstance must arise from some
cause which does not immediately appear; *Roman Catholic faith does not induce
poverty, neither does poverty lead to the creed of the church of Rome;* the
poverty of the Roman Catholics is too general to be accidental, and it should seem
that *it can only have arisen from the deprivations of property to which the Catholics
in Ireland have, at different times, been subjected,* and the discouragement which
the laws till lately have offered to the accumulation of property by Catholics,
and which discouragement is not yet wholly removed. If this be correct, it seems
to result as a duty to those who have to form economical arrangements of a public
nature, *not to make any distinction between their dependents, who are equally loyal,
though they may entertain different creeds,* and that every encouragement which
is held out to persons of one religious persuasion, should be equally held out to
persons of every other religious persuasion; *that every man should look to his*

have endeavoured to give an idea of in the preceding chapter, it would have been inconsistent not to connect some equally provident measures, with respect to Education. Our statesmen well knew that an early culture of the mind alone

> Emollit mores nec sinit esse feros :

or, in other words,

> Learning alone the heart with virtue stocks,
> And hath, like music, power to " *soften Rocks*."

Accordingly they set about reducing us to as minute a minimum in Education, as we had, under their wise laws, attained in Property ; and a brief review of the principal steps taken for this purpose, both by Church and State down to the present time, will show with what a steady eye to the interests of the Rock family, this impoverishing and benighting system has always been pursued.

The principal mediums of education through which the Government had to act upon the people, were the Charter Schools and Schools of Royal foundation.

With respect to the former of these institutions, it might have been possible, perhaps, to manufacture the same number of rebels and bigots at a somewhat less expense, but the perfection of their machinery for the purpose is now, I believe, acknowledged on all sides.

These Charter schools, under the general name of the Incorporated Society, were founded under George II., in the year 1733, for the professed object of " teaching the children of the Popish and other natives ;—and had they suffered us youth of the Roman faith, to drink at the same spring of instruction with our little Protestant fellow-countrymen, without insulting or interfering with the religion we brought from home with us, there is no saying to what an alarming degree of amity the two religions might have been brought in time. Nay, there was even an opportunity for trying the experiment, whether a Catholic could be turned into a Protestant without the employment of actual force.

But our Irish rulers have always proceeded in proselytism, on the principle of a wedge with its wrong side foremost. It was soon found by the Catholic parents, who had intrusted their children to these Protestant institutions, that hatred to their religion was the chief actuating motive of its directors ; and that, like Vathek, when

neighbour's opinion with a consideration that, perchance, his neighbour may be right, and he himself in error."

These two Reports do the highest honour both to the persons who drew them up, and the Company by whom such enlightened persons were employed. Let Irish landlords and Irish secretaries read them, and blush!

he seduced the fifty little ones to the brink of the chasm, in order to hurl them in as a sacrifice to the Giaour, the incorporated Society but took possession of those children, for the purpose of plunging them headlong into Protestantism—a creed, unknown to them but by the Spirit of persecution that dwelt in it, and by the voracity for fresh victims with which that Spirit, like the Giaour, had always cried out from the chasm, " more, more ! "

It may easily be imagined with what horror this design was regarded by a people, who looked upon their faith as the only treasure and consolation left them, and whose tenacity in that faith had been tried by sword, famine, and fire for centuries. Too indigent, however, to procure instruction in any other way, and the laws forbidding persons of their own persuasion to teach, some wretched parents, anxious at all risks to educate their children, continued to let them drink at this dangerous source—with the same trembling apprehension, with which the people of the East visit those fountains supposed to be the haunt and ambush of banditti, and on some of which are inscribed the warning words " Drink and away ! "

In proportion to their fears, their hatred, of course, increased—while the children, compelled to act the part of converts while at school, took revenge for this forced hypocrisy of their youth, by a life of open bigotry and disaffection ever after.

Still, however, the association with protestant play-fellows gave a chance of future friendships and connections, which, if they did not end in conversion, at least would lead to tolerance; and encouraged, at a time of life when the heart is most impressible, that familiar collision by which asperities are smoothed away, and the exclusiveness of the sectarian is lost in the fellowship of the man.

But even this chance, which let in a gleam of light, too strong for the eyes of the Incorporated Society to bear, was shut out by a Resolution [1] of that body in the year 1775, declaring that none but the children of Papists should thenceforth be admitted to the schools [2] —and how delicately they accommodated themselves to the prejudices of these chosen and exclusive pupils, will appear by the following extracts from a Catechism, which they continued to use to as late a

[1] The same policy was pursued with respect to the institution at Maynooth, where it was the wish of the Catholics that Protestants should be admitted on the same footing with themselves; but, this not suiting the good old views of the Protestant interest, it was refused.

In the same manner, in the reign of Henry V. "the Irish students," says Leland, " of the English race who resorted to England for education, were disdainfully excluded from the Inns of Court, by a shameful policy which precluded them from such an intercourse as would have erased their prejudices and conciliated their affections to England."

[2] This Resolution was rescinded in 1803.

period as 1811 , when the recommendation of the Board of education induced them to relinquish it :

" Q. Is the church of Rome a sound and uncorrupt church? A. No ; it is extremely corrupt in doctrine, worship, and practice."

"Q. What do you think of the frequent crossings, upon which the Papists lay so great a stress? A. They are vain and superstitious. The worship of the crucifix is idolatrous."

The courteous address of Launcelot to the young Jewess , " Be of good cheer, for truly I think thou art damned ," seems to have been the model upon which the Protestant Church has founded all its conciliatory advances towards the Catholics.

It may easily be supposed that it was only the poorest and most worthless part of the population, that, with such an insult meeting them on the threshold , would suffer their children to enter these schools; and the few proselytes of any standing that they could boast,—like those *low-caste* converts of our missionaries in the East, whom their fellow Hindoos in derision call " Company's Christians,"—were rare and marked enough among their countrymen , to be pointed out, in the same manner, as Charter-school Protestants.

So difficult was it at last to get up a decent show of pupils—such as might furnish a pretext for those enormous annual grants, by which the Government kept this machinery of demoralization in motion — that it was the practice, at one time, to buy, and even steal little Catholic children, in order to swell the number of recruits for Protestantism, and return annually the proper complement of converts to Parliament.

It will hardly be believed that the Imperial grants to these long-tried nuisances, (whose chief produce of late years has been, according to Mr. O'Driscol, " Prostitutes ' and Orangemen," [2]) amounted for the first sixteen years after the Union, to more, on an average , than thirty thousand pounds per annum ; and for the

---

[1] The privileges of the Ascendancy are , of course, asserted as proudly among this,. as among all other classes of the community—according to the precedent established by " the wisdom of our ancestors," in the case of Nell Gwyn. " When Nell Gwyn ," says Grainger , " was insulted in her coach at Oxford by the mob, who mistook her for the duchess of Portsmouth , (another mistress of that king's, but *a Papist*), she looked out of the window, and said with her usual good humour: 'Pray , good people, be civil, I am the *Protestant* w — e;' and this laconic speech drew upon her the blessings of the populace, who suffered her to proceed without further molestation. " *Biograph. Hist.*

[2] See the Appendix to this gentleman's eloquent work, *Views of Ireland*,—in which there is a mixture of sound sense with rich fancy, of philosophic views with poetic feeling , which realizes fully the precept of La Fontaine , " Que le Beau soit toujours camarade du Bon."

present year 1824, the aid to them from Government, exclusive of their property in lands, and funds, is twenty-one thousand pounds'.

The Schools of Royal foundation are so far more innocent than these "*Chartered* libertines," that, instead of endeavouring to convert the Catholics, the reverend Honourables and Baronets who held the masterships of them, were chiefly employed in converting the funds allowed for the schools into convenient and profitable sine-cures for themselves. Some of these cases of embezzlement were reported to the Government in the year 1796; but the only effect of the discovery was to put a stop to an Act then in progress for the improvement of the system of Public Education;—the persons de-tected in this misappropriation of the public funds, being of that privileged class, into whose pockets, however filled, it has been at all times profanation to pry. Under the administration, however, of the Duke of Bedford (who was not equally inclined to subscribe to that first of the thirty-nine articles of Irish Protestantism—Job-bing), the inquiry was resumed, and a Commission established, which has had the singular felicity of being in some degree use-ful ².

These Royal Free-schools are, it seems, endowed with estates, to the extent of thirteen thousand six hundred and twenty-seven acres; and so well had the Honourable and Reverend masters suc-ceeded in appropriating the chief benefit of the Fund to themselves —that, according to the House of Commons' Report, in 1809, out of the small number of children educated in these schools altogether, there were not above thirty who did not pay as much for their education, as if the thirteen thousand six hundred and twenty-seven acres were wholly out of the question.

From the Report of last year upon the state of these Schools, they appear to be at present rather schools of litigation than of learning —as their returns relate almost wholly to the progress of their law-suits with their tenants, which seem as numerous and as successful as those of Sir Condy Rack-rent, who "lost every one of his suits but seventeen." The Commissioners, however, tell us consolingly, "we look forward to the period when this Board shall be enabled to give its undivided attention to the system of education, without being embarrassed with subjects of finance."

---

¹ We are assured by the Fourteenth Report of the Board of Education, that a considerable improvement has taken place in the Charter Schools; but the remem-brance of their Catechism, and the occasional stretching out of their old claws of proselytism, will long make them too odious to be any thing but mischievous.

² The Fourteenth Report of the Commissioners is full of good sense and libe-rality: and the letter of Mr. Leslie Forster in the Appendix is entitled to the same very rare character.

We now come to the share which the Church has taken in the instruction of the people.

Whatever motives the Government may have had, for exhibiting Education always in the shape of either a bug-bear or a job, it might have been supposed that the Clergy, at least, would wish to see a humanized population around them ; and that those Free-Schools— one of which every Diocese is by an act of Elizabeth bound to maintain at its own expense —would have been cherished with a care and liberality of contribution, even beyond what the provisions of the statute enjoin.

But, unluckily, from some occult cause (for the Commissioners say it must not be attributed to " the backwardness or inattention of the Bishops or Clergy ") the contributions of the Church to this truly sacred purpose have been almost nothing. Indeed, such is the mysterious incapacity of contribution under which they labour, and which might tempt malicious persons to suppose that the " Nolo " of an Irish bishop is reserved for occasions of charity alone, that, at the time when the Report which I have just cited was made, the whole number of effective schools in all the Dioceses together was only 13—And, lest even *this* should prove too heavy " a tax upon the clergy," the Government has, in pursuance of the recommendation of these same Reporters, caused, in several instances, two or more Dioceses to be formed into one district, and appointed but one School to be maintained by the entire Clergy of the Dioceses so united.

Thus ,—as in the instances of Raphoe, Kilmore, and Clogher, which are by the new regulation consolidated into one district— three Bishops to one School is considered not more than a fair and orthodox allowance ; and (though somewhat resembling, in its division of labour, that scene of O'Keefe's where " four French porters enter carrying a band-box ") is held to be an abundantly adequate return from the Church to the People, for the two millions of acres, and the tenth part of the produce of all the other acres which it derives from them.

But even under this light labour, the powers of the Bishops and Clergy seem to have sunk. In the accounts of the Free Diocesan Schools, laid before the House of Commons last year, neither from the Archbishoprics of Tuam and Armagh, nor from several of the other Dioceses, have returns of any School whatever been forwarded ; and an item or two of the account, as it stands, will show how impenetrably closed the purses of the Clergy are, even to the "Open Sesamé " of the Law.

In the Diocese of Ardagh, the amount of annual income for the maintenance of a school is thus stated:—"twenty-seven pounds, *most difficult to collect*, by reason of the numbers liable to pay it ; part is never paid."

In the Diocese of Elphin, the annual income is stated to be fifty-five pounds, and the fund from which it arises is thus described :— " An annuity by bequest, and a charge on the Bishops and Clergy, some of the latter in arrear, from non-payment of tithes, and the pressure of the times."

In the rich Diocese of Derry, where the income required for the school is near nine hundred pounds, all that the Bishop and Clergy can muster up among them towards that sum is one hundred and ten pounds—the remainder being contributed by the Irish Society and London Companies.

In addition to this establishment of Diocesan Schools which the law provides, and which the Church thus frustrates, the parochial Clergy are also, by the 28th of Hen. VIII. charged with the instruction of the poor; and every incumbent appointed to a living in Ireland, takes an oath to the following effect : " I, A. B. do solemnly swear, that I will teach or cause to be taught within the said vicarage or rectory, one school as the law requires."

Oaths, however, are just as inefficient as acts of Parliament. " No school—no scholars " was the return made to the House of Commons last year from the great majority of the parishes; and, even where parochial schools do exist, they seem by these accounts to be supported by every body and by any body but the Clergy—who while they impute to Catholics a laxity in the observance of oaths, exhibit a well-bred indifference about their own, which is, at least, equally edifying.

It must have been a consciousness of the immoral influence of such an example, that induced the Commissioners of Education, in their Eleventh Report, to suggest that " it might deserve consideration, whether the oath should continue to be administered, or whether the Clergy ought not to be relieved from the obligation thus imposed upon them."

There is one mode, indeed, by which these Reverend Gentlemen quiet their consciences, which is too characteristic and amusing not to be noticed. It seems that the sum required as the annual contribution of the clergyman to the parish school, was rated in the time of Henry VIII. at forty shillings. Without any regard, therefore, to the change which has taken place in the value of money since, they consider themselves perfectly acquitted of their obligations, in devoting two pounds of their large incomes to the same important purpose now; and we find, in numerous instances, among the items of the fund from which the school is maintained, " Two pounds per annum paid by the rector."

Even from such a benefice as that of Maghera, the certified value
of which is one thousand eight hundred and seventy-five pounds
per annum, the overflowings of clerical benevolence do not exceed
the ancient modus of forty shillings; and the remainder of the fund
for the support of the school is made up of donations from different institutions, and the annual contributions of the scholars
themselves.

In the great majority of parishes, however, there are, as I have
already remarked, no Free-schools at all. In the diocese of Cloyne,
in which there are fifty-eight benefices, valued, according to an
accurate return in 1809, at forty thousand pounds a year, there are
only twenty schools; and the Archbishopric of Tuam, in which
there are twenty-four benefices, comprising eighty-nine parishes,
has not been able to contribute to the cause of education more than
six schools.

In the mean time, the incumbents of these neglected parishes,
who are many of them non-residents, may be found at Bath and
Cheltenham, effacing the remembrance of their oaths in those Le-
thean waters, and whiling away the time in prospective dreams of
better benefices—like those souls on the banks of the ancient Lethe,
whom Virgil describes as waiting for the fresh bodies, into which
they were to be inducted,—

> ——animæ, *quibus altera fato*
> *Corpora debentur*, Lethæi ad fluminis undam
> Securos latices et longa oblivia potant.

From all this, it will be seen, that if the poor of Ireland had only
the Government and the Clergy to trust to for education, their ignorance would have been as complete as even a philosopher like
Mr. Bankes could require—and the reader of the foregoing statements will, I have no doubt, agree with me, that never did Church
and State, those inseparable companions (so aptly compared to the
twins of Heraclitus, that wept and laughed, waked and slept, and
performed all the functions of life together'), exhibit in any other instance such a perfect co-operation and sympathy, as in this one,
uniform, and consistent task of strengthening the interests of the
Rock family in Ireland, by benighting, beggaring, and brutalizing
the Irish people, under every reign, and in every possible way, that
their joint Excellencies, Reverences, and Graces could devise.

Within these few years, some charitable and well-intentioned
persons, observing how ill our education prospered in the hands of
the Government and Clergy, have associated themselves in various
plans for our civilization and improvement—and the consequence
is, I have, at this moment, arrayed against me, the Kildare Street
Society, the London Hibernian Society, the Irish Society, and a host

of other minor societies, all armed with bibles, religious tracts, etc. determined to put down the ROCK interest, and to repair the mischief so elaborately brought about by our rulers, both lay and spiritual.

To " unwind a wrong knit up so many years," is no such easy matter ; and there is , in some of the prominent features of this new generation of Societies , a family resemblance to the old Charter-school system , which prevents me from feeling any considerable alarm as to their success.

As if we wanted any assistance in perpetuating national differences, one of these Societies has kindly taken the Irish language under its protection ; and the old Milesian vocabulary, which used to be hang-ing-matter some sixty years since, is now—as a preparation, I pre-sume, for the re-enactment of the Penal Code—to be made a chief part of our national education, and to " speed the soft intercourse " of Rockism in future, under the special patronage of " the Irish Society."

The " Kildare Street Society " is also , I find , assisting my inte-rests. Out of the public funds granted to this institution for the purposes of education , the greatest portion , it seems, finds its way to the favoured region of Ulster,—that being (according to the usual rule for appropriating money in Ireland) the part of the country where such assistance is least wanted. By their own report, indeed, it appears that one northern county, Antrim , has shared twice as much of their assistance as the whole province of Connaught , and, in conformity with this system , we find, out of a list of one hun-dred and twenty-seven schoolmasters appointed by them, no more than forty-nine Catholics.

But the " London Hibernian Society " promises to be the most useful to me of any—as the following specimens of their success in proselytism, extracted from the Appendix to their Report of last year, will prove.

In a letter from one of the travelling agents , employed by this body, we find the following description of a little fourteen-year-old Protestant, which he had just succeeded in making :—"Her de-meanour and conversation has gained the attention of her parents to the word of God ; and *although her dissent from the prevailing religion has subjected her to some obloquy and reproach , she* is generally respected by her neighbours, *and at an age little above fourteen , is found the avowed advocate of christianity in its scriptural character,* in opposition to the corrupt glosses and traditions of men."

It appears by the following extract, that proselytes are sometimes promoted into schoolmasters—in the hope, no doubt (from a *London* estimate of the Irish character), that such tame converts will act as decoys to catch others :—" B——, master of our school in

E———, had some time since informed me, that he found in the conversation of a shoe-maker in that neighbourhood, much to strengthen and animate him in his Christian course, and that *they were mutual supports to each other, beneath the trials to which* their *apostasy from popery exposed them.*"

We have afterwards a story, from one of these agents, of a Catholic, who in going through some act of penance with about " fifty fellow-sinners," was suddenly struck with the conviction, that " he was, in the exercise in which he was engaged, adding sin to sin—idolatry to his other crimes." Beneath this impression, adds the agent, "he sunk to the earth nor could proceed, when, as with the rapidity of lightning, a certain text of scripture struck upon his recollection. For some time he was motionless with delight and astonishment : believing, he rejoiced with exceeding great joy; when recollecting the situation in which he was placed, regarding its idolatry with abhorrence, he sprang off his knees and fled from the chapel, never again to visit it or bow to a priest."

Such are the inducements held out to Catholics, to be educated in the Schools of the "London Hibernian Society."

The old Charter school plan of alienating children from their parents, may be traced pretty clearly in the following dialogue between one of the Inspectors of this Society, and " a little girl." "My dear," said I, " where did you find this text?" "Indeed, Sir, I have a good Testament, and can read a Bible." " *Is your father a Roman?*" said I. "*Indeed, Sir, he is, and believes every thing the Priest tells him.*"

Little children, as might be expected, act a considerable part in these cases of conversion. " I will relate an instance ," says one of the School-masters of the Society, " of a child *no more than six years old*, who, on receiving a Testament this quarter, threw himself on his knees, and thanked God for the gift he bestowed on him, through the means of the Society."

If any further proof be wanting of the benefits which these well-meaning persons are likely to confer upon the Rock cause, one more specimen will amply suffice : the convert in this case is " a weaver by trade." "It is manifest that God, who calleth men from darkness to light, hath abundantly blessed the reading of that precious gift to him. He spends all his hours in reading that valuable book, which was the instrument of awakening him out of the deep sleep of sin. *His nearest friends are become his greatest enemies : his wife and brother-in-law say that he is religiously mad.*"

CHAPTER III.

Education of the Captain.—Hedge Schools.—Abduction of a School-
master.—Catalogue of a Rock Library.

It may easily be supposed that my Father was too good a Catholic to risk the orthodoxy of the young Rocks within the prose-
lytizing vortex of a Charter School. Our education, therefore, was
imbibed in one of those ancient seminaries, which, like the acade-
mies of the ancients, are held in the open air, and which, from the
sheltered situation they occupy, are called Hedge Schools.

That particular Hedge School which had the honour of educating
me, deserved rather, perhaps, to be called a University—as the
little students, having first received their rudiments in the ditch,
were from thence promoted, in due time, to graduate under the
hedge.

When I was between 13 and 14 years of age, our old school-
master died; and as I still continued, in those intervals of leisure
which my early initiation into my father's calling allowed me, to
avail myself of the instruction of this worthy pedagogue, his death
was to me, as well as to all the other little Rocks, a serious inconvenience. We soon, however, contrived to fill up his place—and by
an expedient which, as it is characteristic of national manners, I
shall, in as few words as possible, communicate to my reader.

A few miles from our village, on the other side of the river,
there was a school-master of much renown, and some Latin, whose
pupils we had long envied for their possession of such an instructor,
and still more since we had been deprived of our own. At last, upon
consulting with my brother-graduates of the hedge, a bold measure was resolved upon, which I had the honour of being appointed
leader to carry into effect.

One fine moonlight night, crossing the river in full force, we
stole upon the slumbers of the unsuspecting school-master, and, carrying him off in triumph from his disconsolate disciples, placed
him down in the same cabin that had been occupied by the deceased
Abecedarian[1]. It is not to be supposed that the transfluvian tyros

---

[1] Lady Morgan mentions a similar circumstance in her amusing " Sketches of
Ireland."

By the following statement from the Accounts relating to Education, laid before the House of Commons last session, it appears that *schools* are sometimes
stolen in Ireland, as well as *school-masters*.—"There are two parish schools in
the parish of Rathcool, one protestant, and the other papist. The papist school-
master obtained a licence thirty years ago under pretence of being a protestant.
By this manœuvre he got possession of the parish school-house and its annexed
glebe, and retains it in defiance of the parish minister, and will yield to nothing
but force. His name is Daniel Brady.

submitted patiently to this infringement of literary property—on the contrary, the famous war for the rape of Helen was but a skirmish to that which arose on the *enlèvement* of the school-master ; and, after alternate victories and defeats on both sides, the contest ended by leaving our party in peaceable possession of the pedagogue, who remained contentedly amongst us many years , to the no small increase of Latin in the neighbourhood.

Such, gentle reader, is the unceremonious way, in which matters of love, law, and learning are settled among us. Whether the desired object be cattle, young ladies , or school-masters , *Abduction* is the process resorted to most commonly. Our rulers having, through a long series of centuries , by indiscriminate confiscations , transportations, and executions , set us the example of a total disregard to persons or property, we have followed in their footsteps with a "desperate fidelity,"—and there is not, perhaps, in the history of the world, another instance of a Government and a People going on so long together, with so little observance of law on either side.

It is, however, a great mistake to say that the Irish are uneducated. There are many, it is true, among us , who might exclaim, like Skirmish , "If I had handled my pen as well as I have handled my bottle, what a charming hand I should have written by this time ! "—but there is no doubt that the faculty of reading and writing is quite as much diffused among the Irish as among the English peasantry.

The difference is not in the *quantity,* but the *quality,* of our education. The Charter schools having done their utmost to sicken us against Catechisms , and our own Priests not suffering us to read the Bible [1], we are driven, between both, to select a course of study for ourselves ; and the line of reading most usually adopted is as follows :—

In History,—Annals of Irish Rogues and Rapparees.

In Biography,—Memoirs of Jack the Bachelor, a notorious smuggler, and of Freney, a celebrated highwayman.

In Theology, — Pastorini's Prophecies, and the Miracles of Prince Hohenlohe.

In Poetry, — Ovid's Art of Love, and Paddy's Resource.

In Romance-reading , — Don Belianis of Greece , Moll Flanders, etc. etc.

[1] The arguments of the Roman Catholic Clergy against the use of the Bible, as a class-book, are well-founded; but the length to which some of them carry their objections to a free and general perusal of the Scriptures, is inconsistent with the spirit, as well of Civil as of Religious liberty.

Such being the leading works in that choice Catalogue, from which, according to the taste of the parties, is selected the chief reading of the Cottagers of Ireland.

So educated [1], and so governed, is it wonderful that the ROCK FAMILY should flourish?

CHAPTER IV.

The Captain's opinions on Tithe matters.—Testimonies in favour of Tithes from the Old Testament.—From the Heathens.—From the Gospel.—From the Fathers.—Civil Right to Tithes.

As Ecclesiastical matters very early attracted my attention, and have formed a considerable part of the business and glory of my existence, I shall not, I trust, be thought to digress unseasonably, in devoting a few pages to the interesting and lively subject of Tithes.

In the *practical* part of Tithe affairs, I am (thanks to my Reverend antagonists, and the *bellum sacrum* that has been so long waged between us) tolerably conversant. But I have also, during those intervals of learned leisure, which a compulsory residence in some of his Majesty's strong places has afforded me, made researches into the history and antiquities of Tithes—with a few of the results of which I shall, as briefly as possible, acquaint the reader.

By most of those writers who have argued for the Divine Right of Tithes, the quarrel between Cain and Abel is considered to be the first Tithe-case upon record—so that bloodshed appears to have been an ingredient in the transaction from the very first.

In a Penitential written for the direction of Priests in Confession, about the time of Henry VI., the Priest, in his advice " upon the point of Tithing ," thus refers to this precedent : " Afterward, Adam had two sonnes, Caine and Abell. Abell tithed truly, and of the best; Caine tithed falsely, and of the worst. At last, the fals tither Cayn slough Abell, his brother ; for he blamyd him, and seyd that he tithed evil. And wherefore our Lord God accursed Cayn, and all the erth in his work. So ye now see that fals tything was the cause of the first manslaughter that ever was."

Other Reverend antiquarians have gone still higher, and assert that Adam himself was the first tithe-payer. In mentioning this wise opinion two hundred years ago, Selden said, " I think that in the time of this light of learning, none have durst venture their credits upon such fancies." But, if Selden had lived in the begin-

[1] Sir John Newport, with whom originated the former Board of Education, has just gained another of those triumphs, which the country owes to his honest zeal, by inducing the Ministers to consent to a new Commission for the same important purpose.

ning of the nineteenth century, he would have found a much more adventurous spirit of absurdity; and in an " Essay on the Revenues of the Church of England , etc. .by the Reverend Morgan Cove , D. C. L. Prebendary of Hereford , and Rector of Eaton Bishop ," he would have read the following passage :—" Nor does there remain any other method of solving the difficulty , but by assigning the origin of the custom (of Tithes) , and the peculiar observance of it , *to some unrecorded revelation made to Adam ,* and by him and his descendants delivered down to posterity."

It has been asked , to what parish church Adam paid his tithes? but the Reverend Mr. Cove has not yet returned an answer.

In general , however, the Tenths paid to the Levites are the scriptural precedent upon which a claim to Tithes is founded ,—in other words, a ceremonial of the Jewish Law, which, together with the other ceremonials of that Law , was set aside by the Gospel , and which the Jews themselves no longer practise , is considered by a *Christian* Priesthood good and sufficient authority for taking a tenth part of the produce of all England and Ireland unto them- selves. If the early Fathers may be accused of *Judaizing ,* what shall we say to this more modern Levitism?

Let it be remembered , too , that, though the Jewish ordinance enjoined the payment of Tithes to the tribe of Levi , *within the land of Canaan only,* these reverend antiquarians do not at all the less gravely quote it, as applicable to their own peculiar pa- rishes and purposes ; and some reverend Mr. O'Flaherty (who is *not* of the tribe of Levi), and who dwells in Ballynakilty (which is *not* the land of Canaan), may yet , perhaps , at this moment, be quoting Leviticus and Deuteronomy, to prove to the Ballynakiltians his sacred right to the tenth ridge of every miserable potatoe-crop within his reach.

If authorities from the Old Testament are to be cited , the best prototype of tithe-takers (at least of Irish tithe-takers) is to be found among those sons of Eli , in Samuel, who struck their flesh-hooks into the pots and pans of the people, and " all that the flesh-hooks brought up, the priest took for himself,"—who said , " thou shalt give it me now , and if not I will take it by force ; " and who at last, by their rapacity, brought these priestly dues into such disrepute , that " men abhorred the offerings of the Lord."—1 Samuel, ii. 16, 14.

Not content with Jewish authorities , the Reverend writers in defence of Tithes have condescended to call in even Pagans to their assistance ; and inform us , with much complacency, that not only the Greeks and Romans, but the Arabians, Ethiopians , Phœni- cians , etc, were all most strict and exemplary tithe-payers.

Hercules, it appears, was a considerable receiver of Tenths; and
if he was also his own Collector, practised as I am in skirmishes with
Proctors, I should hesitate, I own, before I encountered so formidable a Tithe-gatherer.

The story of Cacus, stealing away the flocks of Hercules ', is,
no doubt, an allegory, prophetic of the loss which the Irish Clergy
sustained, in having the Tithe of agistment of Cattle taken from
them by the Irish Parliament. The character, indeed, given of
Cacus by Virgil, represents the Parliament of that penal period, to
the very life—

> At furiis Caci mens effera, *ne quid inausum,*
> *Aut intractatum sceleris dolive fuisset.*

The circumstance, too, of Cacus pulling the cattle by the tail
may possibly allude to the method of ploughing by the tail, so long
practised in Ireland :

> Aversos caudâ traxit in antra boves;

but this I throw out merely as a suggestion.

We are next presented, by these classical clergymen, with an
association between Poets and Tithe-holders, which is as unexpect-
ed as it is edifying. From the lucubrations of the Reverend Mr. Cove
and others, it appears that Apollo, also, was so much in the receipt
of this kind of dues, that one of the epithets by which he was distinguished was δικατηφορος, the Tithe-bearing,—or, as Selden more
fancifully renders it, " crowned with Tithes." ²

This, no doubt, is the secret of that inspiration, which has made
the Church so fertile in good poets at the present day—and, if the
Tithe-crowned Apollo could always boast such votaries as Crabbe,
Bowles, Crowe, Milman, and Croley, even Captain ROCK would
bow the knee to him in homage, and acknowledge his *Tenth* Muse
to be worth almost all the other Nine.

---

¹ According to some accounts (Halicarnass. Ρωμ Αρχαιολ. α.) Hercules himself first spent the Tenth of what he took from Cacus, in a jolly feast with Evander
and his companions—from whence (says Dionysius) originated the offering of
Tithes at the altar which they raised to him.

This jolly method of spending the Tithes is still preserved in Ireland most
classically.

² The famous courtezan Rhodopis used to send annually the tithe of her earnings to Delphi; where, doubtless, the venerable priests of the temple defended
the sacredness of the due with all proper spirit—pronouncing every man an
atheist, who dared to question or even smile at it.

This singular sort of Tithe was not confined to Heathen Church establishments, but, like all other profitable practices, found its way also into the Christian church. "Some Canonists," says Aume, "went so far as to affirm that the
Clergy were entitled to the tenth of the profits made by Courtezans."

When we add to the above classical examples of Tithing, that of the Tenth allotted by Juno to the Priests of Cybele, for the trouble they took in teaching Mars to dance, we shall have done full justice to the argument in favour of Tithes, derived by Church Divines from the religious institutions of the Heathens.

We come now to the Gospel authorities for this practice—and here, at least, we might expect to find its Reverend advocates, armed with such texts in support of their claim, as would at once reduce us to reverential silence, and justify the assertion of Archdeacon Coxe in a late pamphlet, that Tithes " are derived from such a high and sacred source, as no believer in revelation can speak of without respect.".

But, no—on the contrary, all here is silent. Neither from the lips of the Divine Founder of Christianity himself, nor from the pen of any of his disciples, has there fallen a single precept, enjoining the payment of Tithe to any class of priesthood whatever. Out of this sacred region, therefore, I may hurry without another word—happy to find it unmarked by a single foot-print of the Tithe-gatherer, and only regretting that my Reverend antagonists should, by seeking authority for their worldly-mindedness in such sources, make it necessary for unhallowed feet like mine, to follow them so near the confines of all that should be most holy and unapproachable.

In the same manner, though not with the same reverential feelings, I shall pass over the testimonies to Tithing cited from the Fathers—those convenient authorities, whose folios have always served as a sort of spare bolsters to theology, to be placed wherever an occasional support was wanting, and then thrown aside when the purpose was served. Thus, for instance, if Origen, in the simplicity of his benevolence, refuses to believe in the doctrine of eternal punishment, he is instantly and indignantly pronounced a heretic, a blasphemer, and even *disseised* of his saintship for a notion so abominably charitable. But, if the same Origen should recommend, (as he does in one of his Homilies) that First-fruits and Tenths should be duly paid, he is then the very " top of judgment," and is quoted by Archdeacon Coxe and brethren, with all the reverence which an opinion so clerical and orthodox demands.

The brief sum, however, of this part of the History of Tithes is as follows. It was not till the fourth Century that this mode of providing for the Clergy was introduced into the Church; and, even then, the Priest was entitled but to a third part of the Tenths, the remaining two portions being appropriated to the repair of Churches and relief of the Poor. In the course of time, however, the Priest contrived to monopolize all to himself [1], and from that moment the struggle between the Laity and the Clergy began—the former paying reluctantly, or not at all, and the latter cursing them with all the flowers of Church eloquence, in consequence.

The following specimen of the style of malediction used on those occasions, will serve to show what a kindly feeling this Jewish custom was the means of introducing into the Christian Church :—
" Si quis autem hæc omnia non decimaverit, prædo Dei est, et fur et latro, et maledicta quæ intulit Dominus (τω) Cain non recte dividenti congeruntur."

Not only disputes, but bloodshed followed in the wake of this new Tithing system—and the Danes put their king, Knout the Fourth, to death, for no other cause, than having attempted to impose it upon them. [2]

Let us now see whether the Civil Right, on which the Clergy rest their claim to Tithes, is bottomed on grounds more tenable or respectable.

The most ancient law concerning this right in England was made by Offa, king of Mercia—who, having murdered under his own roof, Ethelbert, King of the East Angles, who had come to sue for his daughter in marriage, invested the Church, by way of atoning for this bloody violation of hospitality, with a legal property and inheritance in Tithes.

Such is the origin to which the Clergy themselves refer for the first establishment of Tithes as a Civil right in England—and it is thought by them, at this day, a sufficient reason for taking a fifth or fourth of the rental of all England, that king Offa, in the year 753, could not sleep easy in his bed, without making a present of the Tenth part of his domains to the Clergy.

He was followed by another pious patron of the Church, King Ethelwolf, who, being alarmed by threats of fresh invasion from the Danes, consulted his Clergy as to the most efficacious mode of propitiating heaven, and averting the calamity. The Clergy recom-

---

[1] About the year 1200, we find Pope Innocent III. complaining bitterly of those who were so ungodly as to pay their Tenths away from the Church to the Poor. " Graviter ergo peccant," says his Holiness, "qui decimas et primitias non reddunt sacerdotibus, sed eas pro voluntate sua distribuunt indigentibus." — SELDEN.

[2] It is not improbable that the Danes gave my ancestors some lessons when they were in Ireland—as their method of serving Tithe-owners resembles our own treatment of Proctors most closely. Under King Waldemar the First, when the Clergy threatened to discontinue their functions, unless Tithes were paid more regularly than heretofore, the People answered that they must either do their duty, or quit their country; otherwise (in the true Rock style), " non solum rerum amissionem, sed membrorum etiam truncationem demorarentur."

mended Tithes , as a specific in all such cases ; and King Ethelwolf,
improving on the piety of Offa , who had given them but a tenth of
his own domains , made over to them that proportion of the produce
of the whole kingdom — by the blessing of which donation , as well
as of three hundred marks annually to the Pope, for the purchase
of oil for the lamps at St. Peter's and St. Paul's , he got rid of his
Royal panic about the Danes , found Tithes , as he says in his Charter, " beneficial to the health of his soul ' ," and, like Swift's generous country-gentleman , who ,

> out of his great bounty,
> Built a bridge at the expense of the county,

saddled posterity with the payment of his " soul's health " for ever.
" Thus ," says the Reverend Mr. Cove triumphantly , " were the
Saxon Clergy endowed ² with a legal, hereditary and permanent
right and property in Tithes , by which their successors have ever
since holden them , and by which they are as fully entitled to and
possessed of their tenth parts , as all proprietors of lands are of the
other nine." That is to say, King Ethelwolf gave to the Church—
not the Tenth part of any actual estates or possessions , for here lies
the fallacy under which Tithes are represented as property ³—but

' The same generous motives are professed by King Stephen , in his confirmation of these Grants.—"For the salvation of my own soul, and the souls of
my father and mother, and all my forefathers and ancestors, etc." In like manner, in the year 852 , " Raginer, Duke of Lorraine," says Selden , " gave a whole
town away to the Abbey of Vito in Verdun , with the appurtenances ,. and all the
Tithes of the Land for the health of his own soul, and the souls of his wife,
children , and parents." Most expensive, to be sure, were the souls of Kings and
Dukes in those times. But why, in the name of common sense, should England be
the only country that continues paying for them still?

² The author of the Article on Ecclesiastical Revenues , in the last Quarterly,
No. 50, well aware that this alleged origin of the right of tithes , is , though sufficiently royal, not very reputable, has endeavoured to get rid of the two Saxon
monarchs altogether—and prefers seeking the source of all Ecclesiastical property
in certain grants of private individuals, which, he yet acknowledges, "it is impossible to prove by any existing documents." It would have been wiser, like
Dr. Cove, to hold fast by Offa and Ethelwolf. Besides , the objection to a right
of bequeathing away the results of future labour, skill, expenses , etc. lies, in principle, as strongly against the private individual as against the monarch " If Tithes,"
says an honest Quaker, who has written very sensibly on the subject, " be the
Tenth of the Profit or Increase of the Land, and they that settled Tithes were
actually seised of no other profits or increase , than what did grow, increase , or
renew upon the land while they were actually seised of it. So that such settlement,
how valid soever while they lived, must expire with them. "

³ It is amusing to observe how the word *Property*, as applied to tithes, eludes
the grasp of definition. "This property ," say some of the Reverend claimants ,
" doth not belong to either the Person or the Office apart, but the Property belongs
to the Person as qualified by holy orders , and put into actual possession by insti-

the Tenth part of what King Ethelwolf did not then possess, and
therefore could not grant away; namely, all future profits and
increase upon lands, arising from the labour and skill of husband-
men yet unborn '—or, in other words, a mortgage without equity
of redemption, upon the industry of all future English farmers, for
ever. This, too, because King Ethelwolf was in a fright about the
Danes, and thought the only chance of safety, for either his soul or
his body, lay in filling the pockets of the Priests of England with
money, and the lamps of St. Peter's at Rome with oil.

My Reverend opponents answer (in the same spirit with which
a Priest of Delphi would have defended the Tithe of the fair courtezan Rhodopis) that it matters not what were the character or
motives of the donor — that the grant has been made, and a right
thereby instituted, which, whatever may be the consequences,
"ruat cœlum," cannot be recalled. Where, then, are all the other
wise grants and imposts of that enlightened period—the Peter's-
pence, the Church-scot, the rich endowments of monasteries and
Churches, most of them bestowed for the same laudable purposes,
namely, the health of such souls as Offa's and Ethelwolf's? where
is all this sacred property now? where all the charters, deeds,
seals, etc. by which it was ratified? Gone to the moon — to that
repository of things lost on earth, where Astolpho found the Deed
of Gift from Pope Silvester to Constantine, and where I see no
earthly or heavenly reasons why the Charters of Offa and Ethelwolf
should not join them.

In fact, till the time of Henry VIII. there was no effective statute

tution or induction." To this Ellwood, the quaker already quoted, answers:—" If
the property doth not belong to either the Person or the Office apart, what
becomes of the property when they are parted? where resteth the property when
the office is void? Doth the property cease? They had best have a care of that, for
that will shrewdly endanger their title. "

In a late Manifesto of the Irish Church, entitled "The Case of the Church of
Ireland stated," the difficulty is got rid of by considering every individual Parson
as a Corporation in himself. " Besides aggregate corporations, there are others
called sole, as consisting at a given time of a single individual. By the act of
incorporation, these legal persons, like the former, are exempted from mortality,
and invested with rights as perpetual as their existence. Such is the King, who,
to the Constitution, never dies. Such too is the Parson of every Parish."

The King and the Parson!—The vast "importance of a man to himself," so
happily illustrated in " the Memoirs of P. P. Parish Clerk," is also strikingly exem-
plified in every page of this Reverend Champion.

' " A perpetual grant of Tithes implies a grant not only of other men's stocks,
in which the granters had no property, but of other men's labour, skill, diligence,
and industry also, long before they were begotten; upon which supposition all
men but Priests, since Ethelwolf's time, must be born slaves, under an obligation
to employ their time, pains, industry and skill in working for the Priests."—ELL-
WOOD, *Foundation of Tithes shaken.*

law to enforce the payment of Tithes in England. The Church had, it is true, for centuries before, brought into play the whole battery of decrees, canons and curses, for the purpose of establishing a right to these dues, but the people had never, either by themselves or their representatives, consented to such an encroachment on their property. [1] The exaction of Tithes, therefore, under the authority of Papal decrees, was in no respect different from the rest of those pious robberies, which his Holiness, the Pope, was in the habit of committing on all the high-ways of Europe. It is singular enough, too, that Reformed England should now be almost the only country in the world where this truly Papal impost is still retained. "Apud Anglos (says Gesner) hodie disputatur adhuc an Decimæ sint res juris divini. Nostri Principes in Germaniâ sunt sapientiores; illi abrogârunt eas."

To the Acts, therefore, of the 27th and 32nd years of Henry VIII. the Clergy can alone refer for a legal right to Tithes—and to all the sacredness which the Laws of Henry VIII. can confer on their claims, they are fully entitled.

But the sweeping alienation into lay lands, not only of Tithes, but of all other sorts of Ecclesiastical property, both under this monarch in England [2] and James VI. in Scotland—and the confirmation by Charles I. in the latter kingdom, of the titles of those Barons, who had plundered the "Spirituality" of the Church, sufficiently show how little sacred, in any sense of the word, this species of property has been held even by those, to whom the Clergy look up as their Supreme Heads.

The Ecclesiastics of Scotland, previous to the Reformation, engrossed, in one form or another, half the landed property of the country, and their Tithes alone are said to have amounted to one fourth of the rents of the whole kingdom. Yet, now, so little scruple has there been in getting rid of this obnoxious burden, that they no longer exist in Scotland, as a contribution of the produce of the land; but, assuming the form of a fixed rent, leave the farmer his whole crop to manage as he likes, and the minister his whole time to devote to works of peace and usefulness—no fear of severance to interrupt the labours of the one, nor any decimal calculations to disturb the devotions of the other.

---

[1] See "Reply to Archdeacon Coxe on the Subject of Tithe Commutation by John Benett, Esq. M. P."—a pamphlet, which shows how easily an intelligent country-gentleman may foil even an Archdeacon at his own weapons, and assert the supremacy of good sense over the vain pretensions of learning.

[2] " In the Act of 32 Henry VIII." says Antony Pearson, "Tithes are called Spiritual Gifts; and there, of impropriate Tithes, sold after the Dissolution, it is said *they are now made Temporal;* and, before that time it was never heard that tithes were called a Temporal Right."—*Great Case of Tithes.*

I have thus hastily but, to myself, satisfactorily exposed, the futility of those claims as well divine as civil, which my Reverend Antagonists set up to an inviolable property in Tithes. I shall, in a future Chapter, lay open some of the machinery of the Tithing system—particularly as brought into operation in Ireland, and as connected with the interests and prosperity of my own family there.

Like a physician, who writes a treatise upon the disease by which he lives, without any fear of losing practice by his exposure of its diagnostics, I shall freely point out all the ravages of this Ecclesiastical malady, without much dread of being superseded in my manner of treating it, or of being doomed to idleness by any radical removal of the complaint. The perusal of Mr. Haslam's work on Insanity, has never, that I know of, prevented any gentleman, so disposed, from going mad; and I shall not be surprised to hear of Mr. Wetherell, rising from the perusal of this very Chapter of mine, to state gravely in the House of Commons, that "Tithes are a sacred *vinculum* between the Clergyman and his parishioners, and possess a certain *noli me tangere* quality about them, which makes it necessary to leave them *in statu quo*, and go on paying them *in sæcula sæculorum.*'

CHAPTER V.

1763—1778.

Political State of Ireland during the early part of the Captain's Life.—Dr. Lucas.—Undertakers.—Administration of Lord Townsend, Lord Harcourt, etc.—Corruption.—The "Catholic Enemy."—Jews—Converts.

For about fifty years after the Revolution, there was in the Politics of Ireland no Irish Party. Our Parliament was but a sort of Chapel of Ease to that in Westminster. Irish pensions, Irish peerages, and even Irish patriotism were all exclusively in the hands of Englishmen, or the sons of Englishmen—and, though now and then their deliberations affected to be patriotic and national, the country itself had as little to do with the matter, as a corpse has with the inquest the coroner holds over it.

Even the patriotism of Swift, as I have already remarked, might have come under his own interdict, as an imported article; and,

---

' A faint imitation of this gentleman's learned style of speaking. May I venture to recommend for his perusal the Diatribæ of Bishop Montague on Tithes, where he will find specimens of this *tesselated* style, almost equalling his own? For instance :—" *Scilicet*, you are *gallinæ filius albæ* in your own opinion. But *hæc erat illa Helena*, good master Selden, not as you mistake the matter."

useful and honourable as his genius has been to Ireland, that happy illustration of the machinery of most human motives, " *Une roue de cuivre fait tourner une aiguille d'or*," may without much injustice, be applied to those of Swift—as English discontent was, after all, the " roue de cuivre " that put the " aiguille d'or" of his patriotism in motion.

It was not till about the period of Lord Harrington's administration (1747-9), that the English in Ireland began to be, as Burke says, "domiciliated," and to feel that they had a country—and it is in the writings of that indefatigable Tribune, Dr. Lucas, that the first dawnings of a national and Irish feeling are to be found. No longer circumscribing the Spirit of Patriotism within the wizard circle of the " Protestant Interest ," he was the first member of the Parliament of Ireland, that dared to extend his sympathies beyond the little colony around him, to the great mass of the Irish nation; —and there is one of his Addresses, in which, putting aside, boldly and entirely, the eternal scape-goat of Popery, he arraigns the whole conduct of England towards Ireland, and declares that " the Mexicans were never used worse by the barbarous Spaniards, than the poor Irish had been for centuries by the English."

The duration of our Parliaments had been, till this time, for the whole life of the king—so that the Parliament, which the death of George II. dissolved, had been in existence thirty-two years!— and it was by the exertions of Dr. Lucas, that they were at length, in the year 1767, limited to the period of eight years. But still their dependency on the will of England was so absolute, and all power of originating Bills,—even Money-Bills—was so completely taken away from them, that their deliberations and decisions, except for purposes of corruption, were mere acting and child's play.

In this shackled state our Parliament remained till 1782,—and, among the farces on a grand scale which have been played off before the world, the Debates of such a House of Commons, in the leading-strings of the English Attorney-General, could not have been the most unamusing to an indifferent spectator. The solemn proposal by some patriot member, of a Bill previously submitted to the *censure* of the Privy Council—the appeals to liberty and the Constitution on both sides—the animation of the opposition benches—the agitation of the galleries—and, all this time, a perfect consciousness every where, that the Attorney-General of England could, with a dash of his pen, reverse, alter, or entirely do away the matured result of all the eloquence and all the abilities of this whole assembly [1]!

With a Parliament so constituted, corruption would seem hardly

[1] See Young's Tour.

necessary, but the influence of the Undertakers (as three or four great families [1] were called) had become, at length, so enormous, and so embarrassing to the Government, that it was found necessary to break it down by every mode of seduction and bribery, that intrigue and a Pension-list, expansible *ad infinitum*[2], could supply.

In Swift's time, "burgundy, kind words, a ndcloseting" was the recipe for bringing over refractory country-gentlemen; but something more substantial was requisite now—and Lord Townsend, under whom the experiment was first tried [3], found the decomposition of these parliamentary clans, a process not less costly than it was invidious and hazardous. He seems, however, to have succeeded—particularly with the patriots; and the names of Loftus, Beresford, etc., among the apostates of that period, show the foundations upon which Tory titles and fortunes are sometimes constructed.

Under a subsequent administration (Lord Harcourt's) so little did Court influence mask its operations, that, for the purpose of recruiting the Treasury-bench against the meeting of Parliament, five Earls, seven Viscounts, and eighteen Barons were all made in one day.

This system of government was all a long rehearsal for the Union —that last grand *bouquet* of the *feux d'artifice* of Corruption. But though even thus soon did that " coming event cast its shadow before," the slightest hint of such a measure was received with universal indignation. The people preferred of the two, a bad Parliament to none at all, and the event has shown that they were right. Like Harlequin decapitated, " though his head was no great ornament to him when *on,* you cannot imagine how awkward he looks without it."

All this time the Catholic " Enemy " (as the laws called their own manufacture) went on increasing in silence and in darkness, like that fire which some French philosophers suppose to exist at the centre of the earth,—working its way upward in secret, till it will

[1] The Shannons, Leinsters, Ponsonbys, etc.—so called from their undertaking, under every successive Lord Lieutenant, on certain terms for themselves and their followers, to "do the King's business " (as the phrase was) in the House.

[2] "The pensions then charged upon the civil establishment, amounted to seventy-two thousand pounds per annum. The private revenue of the crown, which the law left at its discretionary disposal, did not at the same time exceed seven thousand per annum, so that the pensions exceeded the fund which could at all be charged with them by sixty-five thousand per annum."—PLOWDEN.

[3] " By his diverting the channel of court favour, or rather dividing it into a multitude of little streams, the gentlemen of the House of Commons were thought to look up to him, not only as the source, but the dispenser of every gratification. Not even a commission in the Revenue could be disposed of without his approbation. Thus were the old Undertakers given to understand that there was another way of doing business than through them."— CAMPBELL's *Philosoph. Survey.*

at last make the surface too hot to hold us. So little were they attended to, except for purposes of persecution, that in a case where one of their body was tried, for having given refuge to a young lady, whom some protestant converters were laying siege to rather violently, it was stated gravely from the bench that "the laws did not presume a Papist to exist in the kingdom, nor could they breathe without the connivance of Government." This is one of those sublime and during fictions, in which Law leaves Poetry so very far behind it—two or three millions of souls " not supposed to exist"—five-sixths of a people alive only by courtesy!

It seemed, indeed, as if these wise legislators had really succeeded in persuading themselves, that Catholics not only went for ciphers in the census of a population, but, like the devils in Milton's Pandemonium, took no room. For, while in every direction this enslaved race was multiplying (contrary to the noble example of the elephant, which refuses to propagate its race in bondage), we find the parliament in such fear of a deficiency of population, as to encourage the importation of Palatines, Hugonots, and even Jews, by every inducement that not only full toleration, but the most lavish grant of privileges could furnish.

This notable and pious plan for strengthening the Protestant interest by a plentiful infusion of Jewish blood, was first suggested in the year 1747, when a Bill for " naturalizing persons professing the Jewish religion" passed the Irish House of Commons, but was lost, I believe, in England. So late, however, as the year, 1796, " all foreigners of all descriptions" (including of course, Jews, Turks, and other outlandish infidels) were invited not only to the benefits of naturalization, but to the enjoyment of all those civil advantages, from which the native Catholic was then, and is now, excluded.

The Preamble of one of these latitudinarian Acts (1780) merits well to be recorded, but as a sample of legislative effrontery, and of that fancy which some tyrants have for showing that they know what is right, merely to enhance their pleasure in doing all that is wrong: " *Whereas the increase of people is a means of advancing the wealth and strength of any nation;* and whereas many foreigners and strangers, from *the lenity of our government, the benefit of our laws,* the advantages of our trade, the security of our property, and the consideration of the plentifulness of all sorts of useful and profitable commodities, with which Irelnad abounds, might be induced to settle in the kingdom, *if they were made partakers of the advantages and privileges, which the natural-born subjects* of this realm do enjoy," etc.

It is evident that, under Lord Townsend's administration, Patriotism was a much more formidable thing than popery, as, in buying up the former article, no expense was spared,—while the addition of ten pounds to the annual sum of thirty, secured by the 8th of Anne to every Popish priest that should become Protestant, was all that the favourite old cause of Proselytism could obtain. As the Act itself piteously recites, "It was found by experience that the former provision of thirty pounds was in no respect a sufficient encouragement for Popish priets to become converts;"—therefore, what neither thirty pounds nor some centuries of persecution could effect, it was thought a bidding of ten pounds more might perhaps bring about. It was ordered, too, that the forty pounds annually should be "levied on the inhabitants of the district wherein the convert last resided;" and thus the same mode since adopted to check the practice of illicit distillation, namely, that of fining the town-land where an illicit still was found, was by this sagacious Act applied to encourage the growth of conversion—as if it was necessary to add fiscal to spiritual considerations, to keep a neighbourhood on the alert against the introduction of Protestantism among them.

Such (I again and again repeat it) were the bungling bigots and oppressors, whose handy-work we see before us in the present condition of Ireland—whose wicked absurdity still lives among their worthy Orange successors—and whose system will, I foresee, like the old Bucentaur of Venice, be carefully kept together in patched-up preservation, as long as a single fragment of the rotten but sacred hulk remains.

CHAPTER VI.

Relaxation of the Penal Code.—Alarm of the Rocks thereat.—Flattering confidence of my father in the English Government.—His sagacious speech to his children thereon.—Standing toast of the Rock family.

ABOUT this time there were symptoms of a disposition in our rulers to soften the severity of the Penal Code, which alarmed some members of my family considerably. Recollecting those lines of the prophecy, already quoted,

> As long as Millions shall kneel down
> To ask of Thousands for their own,
> While Thousands proudly turn away,
> And to the Millions answer "Nay,"
> So long the merry reign shall be
> Of Captain Rock and his Family,

they considered every approach to justice and liberality, as a step towards the discomfiture and downfall of our Dynasty.

The indulgences, it is true, were not of a very alarming description; for the first great favour granted to the Catholics was an Act empowering them to take leases of " unprofitable bog, "—half an acre of arable land being thrown in as a douceur with fifty acres of bog, "in case the depth of the bog from the surface, when reclaimed, should be four feet at least." This liberal extension of the blessings of property to the Papists, though violently opposed, as a measure tending to encourage Popery, (reclaiming bogs an encouragement to Popery!) was at length carried in the year 1772.

The next great benefit bestowed upon the Catholics was the allowing them to take the Oath of Allegiance : and this kind permission to the victim to come and swear eternal fidelity to his tormentors, —though as insulting a piece of mockery as can well be imagined, —was received with the warmest gratitude by the Catholics ; because it, at least, acknowledged their existence as subjects, and put an end to that lively fiction of the law, which would have returned " non est inventus " of two millions of people.

At length, in the year 1778, the fears of England—then suffering, in America, for her Saturnian propensity to devour her own offspring—and the gradual increase of a national spirit in Ireland, concurred in removing the most obnoxious of the Penal statutes, —of those laws, which had so long excluded the great majority of the nation from all interest or property in the soil on which they trod ; and by which our rulers, having first plundered us of the estates and possessions of our forefathers, set an interdict on our acquisition of any more for our descendants.

By the 17 and 18 of George III., any Catholic, subscribing the Oath of Allegiance and Declaration prescribed by a former Act, might take, enjoy, and dispose of a lease for 999 years, certain, or determinable on the dropping of five lives ; their possessions were in future to be descendible, devisable, or alienable, as fully as if belonging to any other of His Majesty's subjects : nor could a son any longer fly in the face of his father, and by a pretended conformity to the established faith, despoil him at once of all right in the disposal of his property, and bring his grey hairs in sorrow and beggary to the grave. [1]

---

[1] The relaxing laws of this period, however, only related to *real estates* and *chattels real*, and did not affect *goods* or *personal chattels;* so that a child might still plead the Statute against his father in all cases connected with the latter sort of property: and the power with which this parricidal law armed the child against the parent may be judged of from the following specimen :—"But the policy of the legislature was not yet exhausted ; because there was a possibility that the parent, though sworn and otherwise compellable, might by false representations evade the discovery of the ultimate value of such property on the *first* Bill,—*new*

7

Such reverence had the Romans for the deity who presided over Property, that, in making room for the temple of Jupiter Olympius in the Capitol, the seat of every god, except Terminus, was removed. Though our Irish legislature had never, heaven knows, shown any such scruples about this deity, but had shouldered him out of his place for every " malus Jupiter " that came, this first, late sacrifice at his shrine must be allowed its full share of importance ; and the prospect of comfort and security, which it opened upon the Catholics, was viewed with alarm not only by the High-Church politicians of the day, but (as I have already observed) by some of the leading members of my own family—whose coincidence, indeed, with the views and sentiments of this High-Church party is, on most occasions, strikingly remarkable.

Being well aware that peaceful and comfortable habits always follow in the train of competence and security, my worthy relatives naturally feared that the rank and influence of our family might, in the long run, be materially diminished, and perhaps ultimately destroyed, by the spread of such tame and anti-Rockite propensities. Looking, too, upon this measure as but the precursor of more important concessions, which might gradually raise the Catholics to a level with their Protestant fellow-subjects, and leave them at last so entirely without any cause of complaint, that a rebellion could not be had for love or money—they began to regard the " latter days " of the Rocks as near at hand, and fell for some time into a state of despondency, which rendered the spirit of White-boyism in the South very slack indeed.

My father's views of the matter, however, were far more conso-

---

Bills may be brought at any time, by any or by all the children, for a further discovery. Such property of the parent is to undergo a fresh scrutiny, and in consequence of this scrutiny, a new distribution is to be made ; the parent can have no security against the vexation of reiterated Chancery suits, and continual dissection of such his property, but by doing, what it must be confessed is somewhat difficult to human feelings—by fully and without reserve abandoning such property (which may be his *whole*) to be disposed of at the discretion of such a court in favour of such children. Is this enough, and has the parent purchased his repose by the total surrender for once of such effects? Very far from it ; the law very expressly and carefully provides that he shall not ; for, as in the former case a concealment of any part of such effects is made the equitable ground of a new Bill, so here any *increase* of them is made a second ground of inquiry ; for the children are authorized, if they can find their parent has by his industry, or otherwise, acquired any property since their first Bill, to bring others compelling a fresh account and another distribution. They may bring such Bills *toties quoties*, upon every improvement of such property by the parent," etc. etc. *Introduction to a Digest of the Popery Laws*, by the Hon. Simon Butler.

When it is recollected that such monstrous laws were in force so late as the year 1792, can we wonder that a Government by Insurrection-Acts has not yet been able to efface the recollections of them?

latory, and his dependence on the future injustice and absurdity of our rulers much more sanguine. " I grant you ," he would say in Irish—for he never deigned to use any other language to his children—" I grant you, that if the Government were likely to follow up, with a willing spirit, this first step of liberality towards Ireland, and to remove cordially, and at once, every link of her irritating chains from her, the future history of the Rocks would be a dreary and inglorious blank.

" But there is no fear, my children, of such a deviation from the usual course of nature, as a wise and liberal administration of the government of Ireland would exhibit ; and even did the Protestant Church condescend to work miracles, this is the very last she would willingly have a hand in. No, no—it may possibly happen again, in some moment of embarrassment and weakness like the present, that a few further concessions may be wrung from the fears of our rulers : but the very circumstances under which such boons are extorted, leave the giver without merit, and the receiver without gratitude ; and the old system of exclusion and oppression under which our family have so long prospered, will—instead of suffering any material interruption by these momentary aberrations into justice —rather return to its iniquities with a refreshed spirit, and take revenge for the loss of those few instruments of mischief which it surrenders, by a doubly vigorous use of the many that will still remain in its hands.

" So far, indeed, (continued my father,) from foreseeing any mischief to the Rock cause, in these partial measures of enfranchisement which our rulers so reluctantly grant, it is the very mode of proceeding, which, had I the means of influencing their councils, I would myself suggest for the perpetuation of that discord which is so dear to us. Give the Catholic (I would say) just enough of liberty and power, to inspire him with pride and make him feel his own strength ; while, at the same time, you withhold all that could gratify this pride, and employ the strength which you have bestowed upon him *against;* instead of *for,* you. In short, loosen his chains no more than will enable him to be pugnacious with effect, and leave him nothing to be grateful for, but the power of doing you mischief.

" This, my dear children, is the very plan I would myself recommend, for keeping the flame of discord as lively among us, as the inextinguishable fire of St. Briget at Kildare. Under the Penal laws we were benighted and hopeless—complete Enfranchisement would make us enlightened and satisfied ;—it is only in the twilight state between, that those false lights and spectral appearances are abroad, by which men's optics are deceived, and their imaginations led astray ;—it is only after having tasted the cup of liberty, without being suffered to allay our awakened thirst, that that feverish and almost maddened excitement comes on, which is so favourable to the views of our ancient family, and which the Government—take the word of old Captain ROCK for it — will long cherish and keep alive for our advancement and honour.

"Instead, therefore, of seeing in their present measures, any cause for the slightest despondency or alarm, we should, on the contrary, be most grateful for this admirable plan which they have adopted, of increasing the wealth and spirit of the Catholic, and, at the same time, keeping the ancient stock of his discontent and hostility undiminished—of placing him with a sword in one hand, and a hand-cuff on the other, in order that he may be incessantly reminded of his servitude and his strength, and, between both, be kept in a perpetual struggle.

"Let us hope, my sons, for this system the same success, which has attended all others, of a like tendency, pursued by our pains-taking rulers, and let us still continue to drink with the same cordiality as heretofore,—to '*that best friend of the* ROCK *Interest* the Protestant Ascendancy of Ireland.'"

So saying, my venerable father would toss off a bumper of usquebaugh, which was at that time his favourite beverage ';—and never, I believe, was toast drank with a more loyal sincerity, or with more perfect consciousness, on the part of the drinker, of the great advantages derived from the system which he thus solemnly commemorated.

By such speeches as these (and time has fully proved their sagacity and their truth) the hopes of my father's family and followers were by degrees reanimated, and their confidence in the future incapacity and perverseness of our rulers restored.

Nor was it long before the Government itself took steps to undeceive any simple and short-sighted persons, who might have supposed that the reign of terror was drawing to a close. Just at the time when the long-enjoyed sport of hunting Catholics with Penal statutes was given up, a new pack of laws was put into training, of the very same blood-hound breed of legislation—which, under names as various as those of Actæon's kennel in Ovid (Whiteboy Acts, Riot Acts, etc. etc.), have kept the same game full in view

---

' In Foote's farce of The Orators, there is an unanswerable speech by an Irishman in favour of usquebaugh *versus* porter. "As for porter, (he exclaims), if 't was n't for the hops and the malt, I'd as lief drink Thames water." This is like saying, "If it was not for Mr. Canning's fine fancy, abundant wit, felicity of diction, and gracefulness of delivery, I would as soon listen to Sir Thomas Lethbridge."

ever since—thus contriving, with a care equal to that of the Game
Laws in England, to preserve to our Orange country-gentlemen
their right of a Catholic *chasse*, uninterruptedly, though under
different forms, down to the present day [1].

CHAPTER VII.

1782.

Irish Revolution of 1782.—Symptoms of Degeneracy in the Captain.—
Confession of his Weakness.—Wise Speech of Old Rock.—His Death
and Character.

I WAS in my twentieth year at that memorable period, when the
light that had arisen in America found its way to the shores of Ireland—when the Irish Parliament, in the very grave of its corruption, for the first time heard the sacred voice of Liberty, saying,
" Come forth; " and the same warning voice said to England,
" Loose him, and let him go."

Powerful as England had always been in oppressing, she was
now too weak to protect us, when menaced with invasion by France;
and the Volunteers of Ireland took the defence of our coasts upon
themselves. From being the defenders of their country's shores,
they soon rose to be the assertors of her rights; and with swords in
their hands and the voice of Grattan sounding in their van—" my
lightning thou, and thou my thunder "—achieved that bloodless
conquest over the policy of England, whose results were Freedom
to our Trade and Independence to our Parliament.

And here—as a free confession of weaknesses constitutes the chief
charm and use of biography—I will candidly own that the dawn of
prosperity and concord, which I now saw breaking over the fortunes of my country, so dazzled and deceived my youthful eyes, and
so unsettled every hereditary notion of what I owed to my name and
family, that—shall I confess it?—I even hailed with pleasure the
prospects of peace and freedom that seemed opening around me;
nay, was ready, in the boyish enthusiasm of the moment, to sacrifice all my own personal interest in all future riots and rebellions,
to the one bright, seducing object of my country's liberty and
repose.

_____

[1] " From the following circumstance, related by the Bishop of Cloyne, as having occurred at this period, we see that a talent for flagellation is not new among
Irish magistrates : —" In the County of Waterford, Sir Richard Musgrave, Bart.
(High Sheriff for the last year) a gentleman of large property, of extensive and
honourable connections, was reduced to the necessity of inflicting the punishment
of whipping on a Whiteboy with his own hand."

This , I own , was weakness—but it was a weakness "plus fort
que moi." I ought to have learned better from the example of my
revered father, who , too proud and shrewd to cheat himself with
hope , had resolved to make the best of his only inheritance, despair,
I might have learned better, too , even from the example of our
rulers—who not only have never indulged in any castle-building
for Ireland themselves , but have done their best to dispel, as soon
as formed, the bright "dreams into the future" of others. But
I was young and enthusiastic, and this must be my excuse.

When I contemplated such a man as the venerable Charlemont ,
whose nobility was to the people , like a fort over a valley—elevated
above them solely for their defence; who introduced the polish of
the courtier into the camp of the freeman , and served his country
with all that pure , Platonic devotion , which a true knight in the
times of chivalry proffered to his mistress ;—when I listened to the
eloquence of Grattan , the very music of Freedom—her first, fresh
matin song , after a long night of slavery, degradation and sorrow ;
—when I saw the bright offerings which he brought to the shrine of
his country, wisdom , genius , courage , and patience , invigorated
and embellished by all those social and domestic virtues , without
which the loftiest talents stand isolated in the moral waste around
them , like the pillars of Palmyra towering in a wilderness ;—when
I reflected on all this , it not only disheartened me for the mission of
discord which I had undertaken , but made me secretly hope that it
might be rendered unnecessary ; and that a country, which could
produce such men and achieve such a revolution , might yet , in
spite of the joint efforts of the Government and my family, take her
rank in the scale of nations , and be happy !

My father, however, who saw the momentary dazzle by which I
was affected , soon drew me out of this false light of hope in which
I lay basking , and set the truth before me in a way but too convincing and ominous.

"Be not deceived, boy," he would say, "by the fallacious appearances before you. Eminently great and good as is the man to
whom Ireland owes this short era of glory, and long as his name
will live among her most cherished recollections , yet is all that he
hath now done but a baseless vision of the moment—like one of
those structures raised by the genii of fable, to show the power of
the spirit that called it up , and vanish !

" *Our work , believe me , will last longer than his.* We have
a Power on our side that ' will not willingly let us die ;' and , long
after Grattan shall have disappeared from earth ,—like that arrow
shot into the clouds by Acestes—effecting nothing, but leaving a
long train of light behind him , the family of the ROCKS will con-

tinue to flourish in all their native glory, upheld by the ever-watchful care of the Legislature, and fostered by that ' nursing-mother of Liberty, The Church '.'

" Let me draw aside, for a moment; the curtain that hangs between us and reality, and show you what are the actual features of the country, in this hour of national jubilee and triumph.

" A Parliament, emancipated indeed from Poyning's law, but rotten to the heart with long habits of corruption, and ready to fall at the first touch of the tempter—a conspiracy against the very existence of this Parliament, meditated even now, in the birth-hour of her independence, and only reserved, like Meleager's billet, till the fit moment of her extinction arrives—an Aristocracy left free by this measure, without the restraints of an Appellate jurisdiction, to give the fullest swing to their tyranny and caprice—five-sixths of the population still shut out from that boasted Constitution, whose blessings, like the ' sealed fountain' kept by Solomon for his own private drinking, are still reserved for a small privileged *caste* alone;—a spirit of intolerance, even among those self-styled patriots, who ' think it freedom when themselves are free;' and who, though standing in the fullest sunshine of the Constitution, would not believe in the *substance* of their liberty, if they did not see it cast a shadow of slavery over others—an Established Church rising rapidly into power and wealth, and wringing her wealth from the very vitals of those, whom her power is employed in oppressing and persecuting :—such are the principal ingredients, of which this happy country is composed at present, and such the materials of future discord, on which the Dynasty of the Rocks may confidently calculate, for the long continuance, if not perpetuation, of their reign.

" Away then, my child, with all this foolish romance, and prepare yourself, as becomes a son of old Captain Rock, for that enlarged arena of contention, into which Government and Church will soon summon you. I have but a little while longer to live in this world; but I should part from it without regret, if I thought I left a son behind me, who would follow worthily in the career of riot which I have marked out for him."

Not long after this, my excellent father died; and it is worthy of record, as a singularity in the annals of the Rocks, that he died in his bed. He had been wounded in a skirmish with some parish officers, who had seized the cow of a poor woman for Church Rates[2],

' So called by Lord Eldon.
[2] "It seldom occurs that the parish officer is not on the walk, collecting what is called 'Parish Cess.' He is to be met with every day, driving some poor man's cow to the pound, to enforce the payment of his charge, which is assessed by

and were driving it off in triumph to the pound amidst the lamentations of her little ones. My father, indeed, succeeded in obtaining one more day's milk for the young claimants ; but the wound, at his advanced time of life, was dangerous, and he resigned his heroic breath on the 1st of April, 1783.

My father's character was an assemblage of all those various ingredients, that meet and ferment in the heads and hearts of Irishmen. Though brave as a lion, his courage was always observed to be in the inverse proportion of the numbers he had to assist him; and, though ready to attempt even the impossible when alone, an adequate force was sure to diminish his confidence, and superiority in numbers over the enemy was downright fatal to him.

The pride, which he took in his ancestry, was the more grand and lofty, from being founded altogether on fancy—a well-authenticated pedigree, however noble, would have destroyed the illusion. He had a vague idea, in which the school-master used to help him out, of those happy days when Ireland was styled the Island of Saints, and when such of our ancestors as were *not* saints were, at least, kings and princes. Often would he hold forth, amidst the smoke of his wretched cabin, on the magnificence of the Hall of Tara, and the wisdom of the great Ollam Fodhlah—much to the amusement, as I have heard, of the second Mrs. ROCK, who, proud of her own suspected descent from a Cromwellian drummer, used to laugh irreverently both at my father and at old Ollam Fodhlah.

I was indeed indebted for my first glimmering knowledge of the history and antiquities of Ireland, to those evening conversaziones round our small turf fire, where, after a frugal repast upon that imaginative dish, "Potatoes and Point '," my father used to talk of the traditions of other times—of the first coming of the Saxon strangers among us—of the wars that have been ever since waged between them and the *real* Irish, who, by a blessed miracle,

---

the acre. The poor peasantry are, as usual, the principal victims; as the cess is levied from the occupants exclusively."—*Practical Views and Suggestions*, etc., by HIBERNICUS.

The same intelligent and useful writer, in complaining of the wretched state of the *Pounds*, in general, says, "There is no public establishment so much used in Ireland as the Pound; and the fees paid to the bailiffs in charge of these for indulgences, or dues arbitrarily imposed, are comparatively considerable. In consequence of ill treatment in those places of confinement, it happens, not only generally, but almost universally, that the cattle are much injured, often depreciated a third or more in value, whereby the poor peasant is made a serious sufferer."

' When there is but a small portion of salt left, the potatoe, instead of being dipped into it by the guests, is merely, as a sort of indulgence to the fancy, *pointed* at it.

though exterminated under every succeeding Lord Lieutenant , are still as good as new, and ready to be exterminated again—of the great deeds done by the ROCKS in former days , and the prophecy which foretells to them a long race of glory to come—all which the grandams of our family would wind up with such frightful stories, of the massacres committed by Black Tom [1] and old Oliver, as have often sent me to bed with the dark faces of these terrible persons flitting before my eyes.

His hospitality was ever ready at the call of the stranger; and it was usual with us at meal-time (a custom still preserved among the cottiers of the South) for each member of the family to put by a potatoe and a drop of milk, as a contribution for the first hungry wanderer that should present himself at the door. Strangers, however, to be thus well received, must come to pass through our neighbourhood, not to settle in it; for, in the latter case, the fear of their dispossessing any of the actual occupants, by offering more to the agent or middleman; for the few acres each held of him at will [2], made them objects far more of jealousy than of hospitality— and summary means were always taken to quicken their transit from among us. When oppression is up to the brim, every little accident that may cause it to overflow is watched with apprehension; but where this feeling did not interfere, hospitality had its full course, and a face never seen before, and never to be seen again, was always sure of the most cordial welcome.

Of my father's happy talent for wit and humour, I could fill my page with innumerable specimens,—all seasoned with that indescribable sort of " vernacular relish [3]," which Cicero attributes to the old Roman pleasantry. But half the effect would be lost, unless I could "print his face with his joke ;"—besides, the charm of that Irish tone would be wanting, which gives such rich effect to the enunciation of Irish humour, and which almost inclines us to think, while we listen to it, that a brogue is the only music to which wit should be set.

That sort of confused eddy, too, which the backwater of wit's

---

[1] Lord Strafford. See the Preface.—EDITOR.

[2] The misery of a tenure at will, where there is no confidence between the landlord and the tenant, may easily be conceived. "On several estates in the highlands, (says Colonel Stewart), tenants neither ask for leases, nor are any given; yet improvements are carried on with the same spirit as on estates where leases are granted. In the former case, much of the confidence of old times remains, the landlord's promise being as good as his bond."—*Sketch of the Highlands of Scotland.*

In Ireland, on the contrary, the tenant is never sure that his little farm will not be *canted,* on the first opportunity, to the highest bidder.

[3] " Nescio quo sapore vernaculo."

current often makes, and which, in common parlance, is called a *bull*, very frequently, of course, occurred in my father's conversation. It is well known, however, that this sort of blunder among the Irish is as different from the blunders of duller nations, as the Bull Serapis was from all other animals of the same name; and that, like him, if they do not quite owe their origin to celestial fire, they have, at least, a large infusion of lunar rays in them [1].

In the rapidity of his transitions from melancholy to mirth, my father resembled the rest of his countrymen. I have seen him and some of my uncles, bending for hours over their spades, with faces where Melancholy seemed to have written "concession à perpétuité"—when, suddenly, one of the party would jump up and fling his spade in the air, uttering at the same time a yell of mirth, which was echoed as wildly by the rest—and instantly the whole party would take to singing and capering, as if that dancing madness, which is said to have once seized the tailors' and shoemakers of Germany, had suddenly come upon them all.

He was a great believer in miracles, both old and new—but the newer, the better; and, though sufficiently alive to the ridiculous on all other subjects, he would listen to any old woman's tale of a wonderful cure, with a gravity of belief, which was by far the greater wonder of the two—nor was it altogether safe for a bystander, on such occasions, to smile. This, however, I look upon as the natural consequence of his political position [2]. They, whom all human means are employed to torment, may be allowed, at least, divine interposition to comfort them; and as a relief to pride, if nothing else, it is a sort of *set-off* for the slave against the insolence of his oppressor, to present himself as worthy of the peculiar agency of Heaven.

Hence miracles have been the weapon of every persecuted faith. The Reformers in Queen Mary's reign had their Spirit in the Wall, delivering speeches against Philip of Spain, and Popery [3]. We have

---

[1] The Bull Serapis was supposed to have been " non coitu pecoris, sed cœlesti igne, sea radiis lunaribus conceptus."

[2] Our rulers are the last that ought to reproach us with either our follies or our crimes:—

> " If I am mad in other's eyes,
> 'Tis thou hast made me so."

" Tous les Ministres de l'État," says Voltaire, " conclurent que le Taureau blanc était sorcier ; c'était tout le contraire, il était ensorcelé; mais on se trompe toujours à la Cour dans ces affaires délicates."

[3] " An attempt was made," says Mr. Southey, " by the Reformers to perform a miracle after the Romish manner, by delivering speeches against the Queen's intended marriage with Philip of Spain, and the restoration of Popery."—*Book of the Church.*

seen, by the Dispositions collected after the rebellion of 1641, how implicitly a Protestant Bishop could believe in Psalm-singing ghosts; —and the French Protestants, at the time of the Revocation of the Edict of Nantz, made themselves as ridiculous with their Little Prophets, their Shepherdess of Crete, etc. [1], as ever my father did in his most cure-believing moments [2]. That learned divine, Jurieu, who was called the Goliath of the Reformed Church, was a most devout believer in these Protestant prodigies, and anathematized all who did not swallow them as implicitly as he did himself.

It is in vain, therefore, to tell us that Folly confines herself to any particular creed—she is no such bigot, but, like Pope's Belinda, "shines on all alike" in their turn.

Contempt of life, which in some places and circumstances is a heroic virtue, has been in Ireland despoiled of all its merit by our rulers,—who have contrived to reduce the value of existence so low, that it passes, like French assignats, for almost nothing. My father, of course, had this feeling in common with the rest of his fellow-slaves; and, rating the existence of others at the same price which he set on his own, played for lives with his masters as unconcernedly as a gambling *millionnaire* would for sixpences.

He could never, indeed, understand the horror that was expressed, at the occasional violences committed by him and his followers, in this desperate game between them and their masters. Regarding his situation as one of perpetual warfare,—there being always two camps in the country, that of the Government, and that of Captain ROCK,—he looked upon all the plunder and bloodshed on both sides, but as the usual and natural result of attack and reprisal between belligerents; nor could be brought to conceive how his defeat of a band of tithe-proctors, or his burning of an oppressive landlord's corn-stacks, was at all different from the surprise of a detachment, or the cutting off an enemy's supplies in regular warfare.

Cæsar is supposed to have sent a million of men out of the world, and Cæsar is therefore a hero—while, if Captain ROCK, in what the laws have taught him to consider as fair fighting as Cæsar's, puts a merciless driver *hors de combat*, or pushes a middleman's middleman off his step in the ascending scale of tyrants, he is a ferocious, brutal and irreclaimable savage. This my father could never understand; and if he was wrong, his betters are to blame, not he.

[1] See Picart, sur les Fanatiques.
[2] Among the swarm of pamphlets to which the late Hohenlohe miracles gave rise in Dublin, there is but one (an "Attempt to explain by natural Causes," etc.) which is at all likely to outlive the occasion that gave it birth. This very clever production is attributed to the Surgeon general, Mr. Crampton.

Voltaire is of opinion that all the united vices of all ages and places would not equal the miseries inflicted by one single campaign. What, then, is to be said of Ireland, whose whole history, from beginning to end, is but one, long, continued campaign—a warfare, too, combining *both* the sources of misery mentioned by Voltaire, since it has brought the vices of each party into play, as well as their swords!

To reproach a country thus trained, with its riotous and sanguinary habits—to expect moderation from a people kept constantly on the rack of oppression, is like Mercury, in Æschylus, coolly lecturing Prometheus on the exceeding want of good temper and tractableness he exhibits—while the only grievance, forsooth, he has to complain of, is being riveted by his legs and arms to a rock, and having a wedge of eternal adamant driven into his breast!

CHAPTER VIII.

The Captain's opinions of Church Establishments in general—of that of Ireland in particular.—Archbishops and shoulder-knots.—Increase of the Catholic population.—Diminution of the Protestant.—Wealth of the Church.—First Fruits.—Church Rates.—Preliminary articles of a negotiation between the Captain and the Church.

"By Jupiter Ammon," says Clincher junr. in the play, "all my religion is gone, since I put on these fine clothes;" and just so has it happened, since the time of Constantine, to every creed that has assumed the pomp and splendour of Establishment :—what it has gained in wealth and worldly power, it has lost in purity and spiritual usefulness.

That principle of exclusion, too, on which all sects are more or less founded, though comparatively harmless when applied to the world to come, is, when brought into play in the concerns of this life, and backed by the strength of a secular ally, productive of no ordinary inconvenience and mischief.

As long as Popery had the whole Christian world to herself, and the same livery of belief was worn by all, this peculiar evil of Establishments had not yet developed itself. But when the Reformation, unclasping the sacred book, invited every man to read it by the light of his own reason, such a multiplicity of creeds and opinions sprung up through Europe, as made the selection of any *one*, to be the sole, exclusive partner of the State, a choice as pregnant with discord as that of the shepherd of Ida himself.

And here began the interminable mischief of Establishments. The Romish Church, strong in primogeniture and possession, held fast by her *majorat* of power wherever she could, and employed all her old inquisitorial arts to maintain it. The Reformed Faith, while professing to stand up for freedom of opinion, still retained the old Popish antipathy to dissent; and when she said, "I leave you free to interpret the Scriptures as you think proper," added, "But I will disfranchise, imprison, and occasionally burn you, if you do not interpret them in the same sense that I do."

Hence sprung those struggles between rulers and their subjects—that war of the two principles, Force and Opinion, which, at first religious, and then, by a natural transition, political, has spread itself like wildfire every where, and is at present agitating the whole world.

From this statement it will readily be concluded, that I consider a Church Establishment eminently calculated to serve the cause of discord, in whatever form it exists, and as it exists in Ireland supereminently so. In all other countries, the laws of reason and nature are so far consulted in this institution, that the creed of the majority of the people has been the religion adopted by the State; and so essential does Paley consider this arrangement to the first object of an Establishment—the religious instruction of the people [1]—that, according to this sensible Divine, "*it is the duty of the magistrate, in the choice of the religion which he establishes, to consult the faith of the nation, rather than his own;*" and—still more strongly to the point in question—"*if the Dissenters from the Establishment become the majority of the people, the Establishment itself ought to be altered or qualified* [2]."

In Ireland, however,—where every thing is done (as astronomers say) *in antecedentia*, or, contrary to the order of the signs,—so completely has this obvious policy been reversed, that the Church of about 500,000 persons out of a population of seven millions, is not only chosen and crowned as the sole Sultana of the State, but the best interests of the State itself are sacrificed to her pride, and a whole people turned into slaves and beggars for her triumph.

The present Archbishop of Dublin, in his celebrated Charge, pronounces the Roman Catholic Church of Ireland to be "a Church without a Religion,"—meaning, I presume, *not* that such names

---

[1] Because, as he justly says, "more efficacy is to be expected from an order of men appointed to teach the people their own religion, than to convert them to another."

Warburton, too, lays down the same self-evident rule, that "where there are several religions existing in a State, the State should naturally ally itself with the largest."—*Alliance between Church and State.*

[2] The Bishop of Cloyne (Woodward), in quoting this opinion, considers it "decisive against the Protestant Church in Ireland."

as Fenelon and Sir Thomas More are to be erased altogether from the page of Christianity, but that we poor Irish Papists, having no well-paid Archbishoprics, are *therefore* without a religion—"That fellow has no soul,—where is his shoulder-knot?"

But what will such haughty Ecclesiastics say, when, by the operation of causes, which seem as progressive as time itself, this people of Catholics whom they insult so wantonly,—whose number is at this moment as great as that of the Protestants of England in 1688, and who are, in spite of misery and Malthus, every hour increasing—shall, like the disloyal waves dashing round the feet of Canute, encroach still further on their sacred precincts—when this Church without a Religion shall have left them a Church without a Laity, and when one who inquires, " Where is the Protestant People of Ireland?" may receive nearly the same answer as that Inspecting Colonel, who, on asking, " Where is the Donegall Light Troop?" was answered by a solitary voice, " Here I am, your Honour!"

The rapidity, indeed, with which the proportion of Protestants to Catholics has diminished and is still diminishing, seems nothing less than a judgment of insulted Nature upon that perverse and vicious policy, which dares to set itself in array against the wants and wishes of a whole nation, and, like the absurd people mentioned by Ælian, who opposed the coming-in of the sea with shields and swords, thinks to stop the great current of nature by means of penal statutes and bayonets.

One of those Reverend Orange pamphleteers, who are at present so busy at their old favourite task, of insulting and calumniating the people from whom they derive their wealth, affects to consider this smallness of the Protestant population as rather a lucky and providential circumstance. " There are," he says, " certain compensatory advantages, which may diminish, if not remove, the regrets of a statesman, that the sphere of the Established Church has not hitherto been wider. It was necessary that the aristocracy of this country—the aristocracy, not of wealth and power only, but of spirit, industry and intelligence—should be entirely devoted to England, and should comprehend, in their love of it, every thing that was English [1]," etc., etc.

[1] " *Case of the Church of Ireland stated*, by Declan." This Reverend pamphleteer has had the sagacity to discover some dark design against Church and State in the following lines of one of Moore's Melodies, which he has thus marked in Italics in order to render the awfulness of the menace more striking:—

Then blame not the bard, if in pleasure's soft dream
He should try to forget what he never can heal;
Oh give but a hope—let a vista but gleam
Through the gloom of his country, and mark what he'll feel.

"Our Church is great, because it is so small—
　Then it were greater , were it none at all.."

And to this Euthanasia it must speedily come, unless , in conformity to Paley's wise advice , such alterations and modifications are promptly made ; as shall , by diminishing its powers of mischief, delay, if not wholly avert , the catastrophe.

In the mean time , if what Tissot says be true , that " tout ce qui hâte les battemens du cœur fait qu'il battra moins long-temps," every violent display of vigour—such as an Archbishop *charging* , at the head of his clergy, right into the midst of six millions of people —or, in a humbler way, a Reverend gentleman , like Mr. Fitzgibbon , ordering a party of soldiers into the church-yard , and attacking at once both the quick and the dead—all such perilous manifestations of redundant vigour ought, in the present plethoric and ticklish state of the Irish Church , to be avoided as dangerous : and this hint, though from an enemy , will, it is hoped, not be despised.

To return to the subject of Population :—Even in the North of Ireland , which was not many years since the strong hold of Protestantism , emigration and intermarriage with Catholics have so far diminished its numerical preponderance, that in many places the scale now leans considerably the other way. About sixty years ago , as we are told in Stewart's History of Armagh , the manor of Newry contained twice as many Protestants as Catholics ; and , at present, the latter are to Protestants , of all denominations, as three to one. In Belfast too , where about the same time back there were not in the town and its neighbourhood more than 300 Catholics , there are now , it seems , at least 3500 , who attend the two Roman Catholic chapels in that town. In some parishes of the North , indeed , the proportion of the Roman Catholics has become almost as overwhelming as in the South ; thus in the parish of Clonmany, in the Diocese of Derry, I find the population rated at 85 Protestants , 40 Dissenters, and 4650 Catholics !

In the South , of course , the disproportion is still more strikingly increasing. According to a return made in 1733 , by the collectors of the Hearth-money, the Catholics were to the Protestants in Kerry in the proportion of 12 to 1 ;—and when Mr. Wakefield visited Kerry in 1808, he was informed that the proportion of Catholics was " as 100 to 1, or perhaps more." The same writer has given the following account of the United parishes of Kilbarry and Donagh-

This is like old Croaker, in Goldsmith's play, discovering a threat of arson in a love-letter: "Blood and gunpowder in every line of it! Little Cupid indeed ! Go to the devil, you and your little Cupid together ; I'm so frightened I scarce know whether I sit , stand, or go."

Patrick, in the county of Meath, " as furnished to him by the Rev.
John Fay, P. P. of the said parishes : "

In 1797,	Protestants	51	Catholics,	3750
In 1811,	do.	15	do.	4120

In the Report of a Committee on the State of Popery in 1731 it
was stated that in the County of Mayo the Catholics were to the Protestants as 12 to 1. " We may very well believe," says Mr. Newenham, " that this proportion has nearly doubled since that time."

It appears by Bishop Pocock's census in the year 1731, that there
were at that time in the parish of Tullaroan, county of Kilkenny,
64 Protestants and 613 Roman Catholics, and in 1818 the numbers
were only 5 Protestants ' and 2455 Catholics. It is worthy of remark,
too, as explaining the way in which this enormous defection from
the Establishment takes place, that in this parish, which forms a
part of the Union of Callan, comprising six rectories and six vicar-
ages, *there is no church*, and that, during one incumbency,
140 persons went over from the Protestant to the Catholic Faith [2].

I could bring many other instances; but these will be fully sufficient to prove that, every where throughout Ireland, by a sort of
natural tendency, the waters on which the ark of the Establishment
rides are ebbing from beneath it with a degree of rapidity, which
threatens, ere long, to leave it dry and motionless [3].

---

[1] See the "Statistical Account of Tullaroan," by the Rev. Robert Shaw, in Mr. Shaw
Mason's Parochial Survey. " There are," he says " but two Protestant families,
consisting of five individuals, in the parish, one of whom settled there only last
summer." We have here, too, a proof of the self-frustrating power, which the
Penal spirit is fated to contain within it. In this very parish, where Protestantism
has thus melted away, " it appears by the old leases, that in the purchases made
from 'the Hollow-blade Company' it was stipulated that *the grounds should be let
to Protestants only*." Ib. See also, for an account of this parish, Mr. Sheffield
Grace's rare and curiously illustrated work.

[2] In relating an instance of a much rarer sort of conversion, that of a Catholic
to the Protestant Church, an Irish newspaper some time ago committed the
following whimsical *erratum :* — "Yesterday Lord Dunboyne renounced the
errors of the Popish faith and embraced those of the Established Religion."

[3] Seneca tells us that when a proposition was once made to the Roman Senate,
that slaves should be distinguished by a particular dress from freemen, it was
instantly felt what danger might arise, if the slaves should by this means be
enabled to number their masters:—"*deinde apparuit quantum periculum immi-
neret, si servi nostri numerare nos cœpissent.*"—De Clementia.

That the same sort of alarm is felt among our Orange masters, appears by the
following extract from a letter written by the late Catholic Archbishop of Dublin
in the year 1811:—"A complete enumeration of the inhabitants of Ireland,
distinguishing their respective religious creeds, cannot be effected without the
sanction or permission of Government, *which the present Administration will not
permit.* The partial enumeration referred to by Mr. Newenham, *excited uneasi-
ness in the minds of the Ascendancy and Orange partisans, who represented them*

With such results before our eyes of the old and long-tried system of Catholic exclusion and Protestant ascendancy, I can only say, "God comfort their capacities," who can hope for any better effects from the same system in future; or who, with a real danger of their own making staring them in the face, can conjure up imaginary ones to divert their attention from it. A sailor, who would first scuttle the boat in which he is embarked, and then lustily cry out " Fire ! " as he is going down, would show just as rational a consciousness of his situation as they do.

Let us now see how the Church, that has the care of these few select souls—these " âmes choisies " of the Establishment—is paid for its important guardianship.

It is by no means wonderful that the startling statements which have appeared, of the enormous revenues of the Church of Ireland, should have been received with some degree of incredulity as well as surprise. When, in addition to her usual share of the produce of a country which feeds seven millions of people, we hear of this Church possessing estates to the extent of two millions of acres— when it is stated, that in one Diocese alone (that of Derry) the Church property, over and above the tenth part of the gross produce of the land, must be worth not much short of three millions [1] — we can hardly conceive it possible that such monstrous wealth should have been suffered by any Government, however absurd, to accumulate in the hands of the teachers of so small a part of the population; nor can well understand by what process, even of Irish exaction, an establishment so preposterously, so insultingly rich, can have been spun out of the entrails of the very poorest people in Europe. Indeed, the old notion of extracting sun-beams from cucumbers, seems rivalled by the art with which this Church has contrived to extort splendour and magnificence out of a population of paupers.

That there has been some exaggeration with respect to the value of Irish Bishoprics, I am not disposed to deny. Mr. Wakefield, and, still more, the author of "The Consumption of Wealth by the Clergy," have needlessly over-stated the incomes of some of these Reverend Personages [2], whose prosperity is already sufficiently florid, without

as records of Catholic numbers to threaten the smaller number of Protestants. A similar enumeration even in a single parish must be conducted with caution and delicacy."

[1] Edinburgh Review.—This of course must be a vague estimate; but when it is considered that the Diocese in question possesses, besides estates in other places, about a third of the whole county of Derry, the value of such an extent of land cannot be much below the sum stated.

[2] The present Archbishop of Cashel, whose opinions are entitled to every respect, and whose candour and liberality furnish an example, well worthy of

8

the aid of any such additional colouring. The suspicious refusal of the Church itself, to furnish a full and regular account of its revenues, has hitherto made it difficult to arrive at much accuracy on the subject; and leaves every statement of the wealth of the Irish Clergy open to the same convenient charge of incorrectness and exaggeration. With a similar feeling, Dr. Beaufort, one of their body, having at first intended, in his Ecclesiastical Map of Ireland, to mark with a particular colour the lands belonging to the Church, found the space through which this sacred line meandered so vast, that thinking it wiser, like Dogberry, to " give God thanks and make no boast," he cancelled this betraying line altogether, and published his Ecclesiastical Map without it.

The returns of Glebe Lands, however, are among the authentic documents before the public, on which a pretty competent notion of the great wealth of the Irish Church may be formed. When to these we add the estimates of their own incomes, brought forward by the Incumbents during the late proceedings under the new Tithe Bill, and fully justifying the high average of 800*l.* per annum, at which the benefices of Ireland have been rated '—when we know, too, that three Archbishops, who have died since the Union (Agar, Porter, and Fowler), have left behind them, though possessing originally nothing of their own, no less a sum than 800,000*l.*—we shall be inclined to conclude that the statements which have appeared, of the immense possessions of this Church, are not far beyond the truth, and may add to the other monstrous anomalies of which Ireland is the victim, that of a Clergy better paid for *not* teaching six-sevenths of the population, than the Clergy of any other country in Europe are for instructing the whole of theirs!

With respect to the way in which this unparalleled wealth is employed, we have already seen, in a preceding chapter upon Education, how few scruples have been felt by either Bishops or Clergy, in releasing themselves from the obligation to contribute to the charges of Public Schools, which the laws and their own oaths so solemnly impose upon them. Their evasion, too, of the payment of First Fruits exhibits altogether—both on the part of the

imitation, to his brethren of all ranks, has in a late Charge endeavoured to remove the impression that exists, with respect to the excessive wealth of the Church of Ireland. His Grace, however, has done little more than refute the errors of a writer already acknowledged to be erroneous, and has left the chief grounds, upon which the received notion of the riches of the Irish Church rests, wholly unshaken.

' According to an accurate return made to Mr. Newenham in 1809, the value of the 56 benefices in the Diocese of Cloyne amounted to upwards of 40,000*l.* a year; and, at the same time, " in the small Diocese of Ross there were eight benefices worth 1,000*l.* a year each and upwards."

Church which profits by such conduct, and the Government which sanctions it—such a magnanimous contempt of justice, consistency, and even common decency, that, in putting on record the examples of dishonesty and rapacity, which have been set before us by our betters, both lay and ecclesiastical, this certainly deserves a high and most conspicuous place.

The First Fruits, it is well known, are the first year's income of every ecclesiastical dignity or benefice—and were paid to the Crown from the time of the Reformation till the reign of Queen Anne, when they were given up to form a Fund for the increase of small livings and the purchase of glebes. Although, in the Statute of Henry VIII., which appropriated these revenues to the Crown, there was a provison made for revising, from time to time, that valuation of ecclesiastical preferments under which they were then paid, this old rate, notwithstanding the great rise in the value of Church property, has continued to regulate the payment of First Fruits ever since the same Clergy, who are so anxious to keep pace with the increasing wealth of the times in what they *receive*, preferring rather to abide by the antiquated valuation in what they *give*.

The consequence of this is, that the Fund in question, which may be estimated in England, I believe, at about 12,000*l*. a year, is found to be altogether inadequate to its purposes; and, unless (as the Bishop of Landaff recommended) a new valuation of benefices is made, and the Bishops and rich Pluralists [1] compelled to pay *real* First Fruits and Tenths, some hundreds of years, it is computed [2], must elapse, before the operation of Queen Anne's Fund alone shall have raised the value of the smaller livings, even a single degree above the starving temperature.

Bad as this is, the case in Ireland is a hundred-fold worse. The valuation of livings at the time of the Reformation having, in consequence of the unsettled state of the country, been effected only in certain parishes, the Clergy have, with their usual adroitness, taken advantage of this omission, and founded upon it, in spite of

[1] The only tax that I know at present upon Pluralists is their being shut up in a room at Lambeth, on receiving a second living, and compelled to write a Latin Essay upon one of four given subjects. This, to some of these Reverend persons, who are just classical enough (like the Divine mentioned by Balzac) to mistake " Seneca de *Beneficiis*" for a work on Church Livings, must be, in no ordinary degree, inconvenient—except that, indeed, criticism is bound to be indulgent to the works of *Pluralists*, on the rule laid down so clearly by Horace:—" ubi *Plura* nitent...... non ego pancis offendar maculis."

[2] Dr. Warner, in the Appendix to his Ecclesiastical History, published in 1757, observes that " it will be 500 years before every living can be raised to 60*l*. a year by Queen Anne's bounty, supposing the same money to be distributed as there has been for some years past."

the positive law, a claim to exemption from the tax altogether ;—
so that, between the few who pay according to the low old rate, and
the many who do not pay at all, this Fund of First Fruits, from
the richest Church in the world, does not average more than 370*l.*
a-year!

Nor is even this pitiful amount always duly forthcoming; for it
appears from the official statement returned to Parliament, that
there was not a single penny paid on account of the First Fruits,
either in the year 1803, 1810, 1814, or 1822.

Attempts have been made to prevail on the legislature to au-
thorize a new and complete valuation, under which, even with
exceptions in favour of smaller livings, this Fund might be made to
produce between 20 and 30,000*l.* a-year. But no:—Such a tax, it
was answered, would be "a hardship,"—a hardship upon that
abstract but sensitive personage, the Church. One of the Members
of the Commission appointed some time since, "to examine and
search for the just and true value of the said First Fruits," when
proceeding lately to exercise his powers, according to what himself
and his legal advisers considered to be the true and express intent
of his Patent [1], was suddenly stopped in his career by letters from
Mr. Goulburn and Mr. Gregory,—informing him, for his edification, that the only just and true value of First Fruits was that which
had been set upon them two hundred years back; and intimating
that, if he persisted in finding out any other "just and true value"
than the aforesaid, he should, for such officious discovery, be
deprived of his Patent.

So watchful a dragon is Mr. Goulburn over the golden fruits of
the Clergy—so anxious is he to keep this mighty reservoir of wealth,
the Church, sacred from all purposes of utility, in its present state
of stagnant plenitude, without a single drain or outlet by which
Charity or Duty can draw off the smallest portion of its sacro-sanct
stores.

In the mean time, for the purposes to which this clerical tax, if
paid according to the intention of the law, [2] would be applied—
namely, the increase of small livings and purchase of glebes—
immense sums, to the amount of more than a million since the
Union, have been granted to this omnivorous Church by Parliament.
The people have been thus doomed to see the produce of such fiscal
plagues as the window-tax, which shut out the air and light of

[1] For the Case on behalf of the Commissioners, the Opinion of Counsel, etc. etc., see Papers laid before the House of Commons in April 1823.
[2] In the course of ten years, ending January 1821, it appears that one Archbishop and nine Bishops paid for First Fruits 1131*l.* 12*s.* 9*d.*; whereas the sum they
ought to have paid, under a fair valuation, would have been at least 30,000*l.*

heaven from their already miserable dwellings, squandered away
in the purchase of glebes, even in that rich Diocese of Derry,
whose Bishop [1] was, in the mean time, spending his enormous
income in Italy, unshocked by the sight of that misery which such
exactions were producing at home.

Is a country, thus treated, to be called " barbarous," because
it rebels? Say, rather, what name would it deserve, if it did not
rebel?

Let us now inquire a little into another blessing, which the
Establishment confers upon us, under the name of Church Rates.

The repairs of churches and all the other expenses connected
with them, are charges to which a Fund, constituted as that of the
First Fruits *ought* to be, would naturally be applied, and, far
from inflicting " hardship " any where, such a just and obvious
mode of lightening the burdens of the people, would in the end
materially serve the interests of the Establishment itself, whose
idle and invidious load of wealth is at present weighing it down to
earth. Not only ought it to bless every opportunity that occurs, of
devoting some of its redundance to useful purposes, but it should
even adopt a form of prayer, like that of Midas, to be relieved, as
much as possible, from the golden plethora under which it is
sinking : —

> meritus torquetur ab auro;
> Ad cœlumque manus et *splendida brachia* tollens,
> *Da veniam*, Lenœ pater, *peccavimus*, inquit,
> Sed miserere, precor, *speciosoque eripe damno*.—OVID.

> Unpitied sinking with the splendid weight
> Of riches, once his pride, but now his hate,
> To Heaven he raised his glittering arms, and pray'd—
> " Forgive, ye Powers, a wretch whom wealth has made;
> And ease, in pity of a sinner's cries,
> This golden malady of which he dies!"

Instead of this, however, through the greater part of Ireland,
scarce a shilling is expended in building, repairing or ornamenting
the Protestant places of worship, that is not wrung, by parochial
assessment, from the unfortunate Catholic occupants of the district.
Excluded, too, by law, from attending the vestries, where these
levies are voted [2] and their applotment agreed upon, the wretched

---

[1] The present Bishop, too, upon being consulted with respect to the poor livings throughout Ireland, could propose no other mode of increasing them, than
" by the bounty of the King through parliament!"

[2] " It follows that, in Ireland, the Protestant parishioners actually enjoy the
privilege of assembling together, under the name of Parish Vestries, *to the exclusion
of the Catholics*, of legislating and imposing such yearly land-tax upon the
Catholics, as they may think proper, for the alleged purposes of building, repair-

Catholic is obliged, without even knowing for what, to pay his last penny to the parish officer — or else to see the cow driven away from his famishing children to the pound. All this, perhaps, for the repair and decoration of some church, whose congregation is as select as that of Swift, with his "dearly beloved Roger," — or else to gratify the architectural taste of some Prelate, like the last Bishop of Limerick, who persuaded himself that he had civilized the County of Kerry by means of ornamental spires [1].

Doctor Darwin had a plan for getting rid of volcanos, by making chimneys in the earth, to let the fire or steam escape : but this scheme of tranquillizing Ireland by means of Protestant spires, erected, as conductors, throughout its most electric regions, is an idea still more original and happy.

It will hardly be believed, that one of the Church Rates levied by rich Protestant ministers upon the famishing peasantry around them, is "for the purchase of elements for the Holy Communion." The Bishop of Cloyne (Woodward), in giving an account of some tithe transactions, which occurred in the year 1787, and in which I recollect having played rather a distinguished part, thus enumerates a few of our achievements in the ecclesiastical line : " They attacked the servants of the Clergy - they demanded of them a surrender of old tithe notes — they intimidated vestries from levying money for the repair of churches, for the payment of the legal officers attending the church, and *for the purchase of elements for the Holy Communion."*

Well might an honest Dissenter, who answered this pamphlet of the Bishop, exclaim, " What !—do the Lords of the land even commemorate their Saviour at the expense of the Poor ?"

ing, refitting, etc., Protestant houses of worship:—and of providing lucrative occupation for each other.

" To accommodate the Protestant carpenter, new seats, doors and other woodwork are voted; to the mason, repairs of walls, or perhaps a spire, belfry, or other subject of employment; to the glazier, new windows; to the clerk, a salary, etc. Thus this Vestry, like an Irish Grand Jury, creates lucrative presentments for its members; and the amount is levied rigorously upon the defenceless Catholics."—SCULLY.

The following particulars extracted from the vestry book of a parish, where a new church was built in 1808, will show the mode in which this tyranny of Church Rates is exercised.

" *Organist*—two first years paid by subscription (among the Protestant parishioners), 30*l.* per annum—third year, subscribers refused to pay ;. on which *a levy was made on the parish, and raised to* 50*l.,* ever since continued. *Parish Clerk*—should be 20*l.,* but was raised to 30*l., with a deputy* at 10*l. Singer*—5*l.*"

Among other charges in the book is " 13*l.* to the Rector for consecrating the church at———."

[1] It is but justice, however, to this Prelate to say that he is at present actively and liberally employed in the improvement of his new Diocese, Cloyne.

An extract from one of the Acts in force with respect to Church Rates , will sufficiently show the "tricks before offended Heaven " which our Protestant legislators play in Ireland.—After reciting that "several parishes are united by charters granted by the Crown, in some of which there are *but very few Protestants inhabiting* , and in others *none at all ,*" it proceeds to enact as "just and proper that such parishes of the said Union as have not any church or chapel, or church or chapel fit for the celebration of Divine service , should contribute to the payment of the annual instalments of the loans granted, and to be granted, for the *building , and rebuilding , and repairing of the churches or chapels of the parishes* [1] *to which they are or may be so united.*" That is to say, a parish where the inhabitants are all Catholics, and which neither has a Protestant church , nor wants one , is yet, in consequence of being capriciously united to some other parish, (for the purpose of forming a rich benefice for some non-resident), obliged to contribute to the expense of "building, rebuilding , and repairing" the church of that parish to which it is so united[2], and in which there may happen to be a few Protestants, to avail themselves of such a place of worship.

As it may be imagined by the reader, that this preposterous enactment is only one of the few remains of that Anti-Popery system., which modern liberality has long disavowed, it is necessary to mention that the Act in question is dated March 1823, and is "*marqué au coin*" with the wisdom of the present Secretary of Ireland.

I have said that our Clergy are paid for *not* teaching six-sevenths of the population—but it will be seen by the foregoing statements, that they *do* teach us some most notable lessons. Of uncharitableness and bigotry they have long set us examples , by denouncing us as idolators and infidels, in their charges , sermons, and pamphlets , and by always voting for the continuance of our slavery in the senate. But the instances which I have just given of their evasion of the payment of dues, which shame alone should have extracted from

[1] Lord Liverpool , last session , in a Debate on this very Bill, said , in answer to a speech full of argument and wit , by Lord Holland—that he "would not enter into the general question of the propriety of requiring Roman Catholics to assist in building and repairing Protestant Churches." This was, at least, prudent in the Noble Minister.

[2] Even in England, such contributions to a church in another parish, though from persons of the same faith , has been considered a grievance. "There was a question made," says Sir Simon Degge, "whether one that holds lands in one parish, and resides in another, may be charged for the ornaments of the parish church where he doth not reside ; and some opinions have been, that foreigners were only chargeable to the shell of the church , and not to bells, seats, or ornaments."—*Parson's Counsellor.*

them, if the law did not say a syllable on the matter, sufficiently
prove that, in our notions of honesty also, we have been indebted
to the same exemplary instructors; and that, in refusing to pay the
various dues exacted from *us*, we but follow humbly and at a distance in the track of our Reverend and Most Reverend prototypes."

The very next time, indeed, that it is my lot to encounter a Parson in the field, I will demand a parley, and propose to him the
following terms :—

"As a preliminary to any pacificatory arrangement between Captain Rock and the Church, it is expected that the latter will begin
by acting with a little of that honesty, which she rather unreasonably requires should be practised by the Captain alone. She must
discharge, in future, those obligations which the law enjoins upon
her, and abandon for ever that old and favourite principle, that payment should, in all cases, come from the Poor alone.

"It appears that, since the Union, 47 episcopal appointments
have been made, the First Fruits of which, if assessed and levied
according to their 'just and true value,' would have amounted to at
least 300,000*l.*,—without taking into account the immense sum,
which the dues] payable from the inferior Clergy would have produced in the same time.

"How much misery, tears and bloodshed, might have been
spared to the wretched people, if these sums had been applied to
the purposes for which the law intended them, and thus rendered
unnecessary a few of those most odious taxes, by which a starving
peasantry is compelled to make up for the deficiencies of a rich but
wilfully insolvent Church—how much odium, ill-blood, and discord might have been avoided, if such a Fund had even been employed towards the remission of those disgraceful Rates, by which
the pig-sty of the poor Catholic is made tributary to the ornamental
spire of the Protestant, and wretches, who are all but starving
themselves, are taxed to provide the Church with sacramental bread
and wine—how far such salutary effects might have been produced,
by a little more obedience, on the part of the Church, to the laws
not only of the land, but of humanity and religion, it is not for
Captain Rock to insist upon at present, in an instrument which is
intended to be neither retrospective nor criminatory.

' It is not at all wonderful that the Church Establishment of England should
feel alarmed at these malpractices of her Irish sister, and should hesitate as to the
prudence of making common cause with her. It has been, indeed, for some time,
a subject of consultation among the English Prelates, whether they would better
consult the safety of their own Church, by taking up the defence of the Irish
Establishment, or by leaving it, as a desperate case, to itself:—and the total
omission of all reference to Ireland in the late Ecclesiastical Manifesto in the
Quarterly Review, seems awfully ominous of the latter alternative.

"But the Captain hereby engages for himself and his People, that—if the Church, as the most considerable and wholesale aggressor, will but take the first step in a return to the paths of honesty and justice, by discharging in future those dues which the law requires from her—he will be most happy, without delay, to meet her on the grand question of Tithes, and on all other matters at issue between them, in such a conciliatory spirit as shall not only facilitate discussion, but lead at length to a complete and final arrangement of all their differences.

"In the mean time, Captain ROCK begs of the Church to accept the assurances of his high consideration, etc. etc. etc. etc."

CHAPTER IX.

1782—1795.

Corruption of the Irish parliament.—Pension-List.—Golden Age of Jobbing.—Achievements of the Captain in 1787.—Assumes the title of Captain RIGHT.—State Physicians.

MY father had predicted but too truly. The light of 1782 soon passed away, and left, in the hearts of those who loved Ireland, only a vague and restless imagination of what she *might* have been.

The British Minister, no longer able to govern us by his Attorney general, was driven to the more circuitous and expensive mode of ruling us by our own Parliament; and a course of corruption was now boldly entered into—a sort of frank, Lothario spirit was adopted by the Government, which seemed to say, "Think'st thou I mean the shame should be concealed?" and which soon succeeded in making political profligacy fashionable.

Had it been a regular trade-wind of Corruption, blowing steadily from the usual Tory quarter, servility would have been at least consistent, and might have even pretended to honesty, on the ground of having but one pay-master. But, just about this time, those Titans, the Whigs, had succeeded more than once in scaling the Olympus of office—and, though speedily hurled down again, they remained long enough each time, to puzzle both patriots and courtiers considerably, and to produce such a confusion in their votes and opinions, as made it no easy matter to distinguish one party from the other.

At length, however, Toryism and Corruption resumed their full and undisturbed empire. A regular market was opened at the Castle, and the price of every service, down to single votes on particular questions, was ascertained and *tariffed* with the most tradesman-like accuracy. So little decency did the Government observe in these

transactions, that the Attorney general (afterwards Lord Clare) did
not hesitate on one occasion, when some of the train-bands of the
Court had joined the Opposition, to hint broadly at the expense that
would be incurred in buying them back again.[1]

A writer on Egypt mentions, as a singular phenomenon, the respect which the Mamelukes have for men who have been *purchased*
—far beyond what they feel for the most ancient nobility. A Turk-
ish officer, in pointing out to him some personage who held an important situation under Government, said, "C'est un homme de
bonne race—*il a été acheté*[2]." What homage, then, would a
Mameluke feel for the "hommes achetés" of the Irish nobility—
many of whom might introduce an auctioneers's hammer into
their coats of arms, so often have they and their illustrious sires
been knocked down to the highest bidder!

During the administration of the Marquis of Buckingham the
Pension List out-stripped that of England by several thousands; and
when at length, under Lord Westmoreland, as a momentary sacrifice to public opinion, a Bill was allowed to pass limiting the grants
of pensions to 1,200*l*. a-year, advantage was taken of the few months
that were to elapse before the commencement of the Act, to grant
pensions to the amount of more than 12,000*l*.—being equal to ten
years' anticipation of the powers of the Crown.

This system was the consummation, the *coronis*, of England's
deadly policy towards Ireland. Having broken down and barbarized
our lower orders, by every method that was ever devised for turning men into brutes, she now premeditatedly—by the example of a
gay and dissipated court—by the encouragement of habits of expense, and the ready proffer of the wages of corruption to maintain
them—so demoralized and denationalized our upper classes, that
perhaps the most harmless part many of them have since played has
been that of Absentees.

The venality, peculation, and extravagance, exhibited in the
higher departments of the state, soon spread through the lower—a
concordat of mutual connivance was established throughout,—and
clerks, with a salary of 100*l*. a-year, entertained their principals
with fine dinners and claret out of the perquisites. In the Ordnance
department, it was found in Lord Buckingham's time, that the
arms, ammunition, and military accoutrements, condemned as

[1] *Half a million or more was expended some years ago to break an opposition;
the same or a greater sum may be necessary now ;"*—so said the principal servant
of the Crown.—*Grattan's Answer to Lord Clare.*

[2] "Ce préjugé," Reynier adds, "est tellement enraciné, que les enfans de ces
mêmes individus n'ont pas le même degré de noblesse avec leur père et mère qui
ont été achetés."

useless, were stolen out at one gate, brought in at the other, and
charged anew to the public account.

Those were the glorious days of Protestant jobbing—for, let it not
be forgot that to this privileged class alone, the robbery of the public has been always specially intrusted—then was, indeed, the
Golden Age of the Ascendancy, when jobs and abuses flourished in
unchecked luxuriance—when salary disowned all connection with
duty, and when Boards of Custom, Boards of Excise, etc., were
merely foundations for the support of a certain number of loyal and
Protestant gentlemen, who would have considered it a case of
"calling out," to be asked what services they performed for their
pay. Ovid has described such an age of gold exactly.

> Pœna metusque aberant : nec verba minacia fixo
> AEre legebantur : nec supplex turba timebat
> Judicis ora sui ; sed erant sine vindice tuti.

Or thus, in English, for such of my Family as Latin may not
suit :—

> How tranquil then the loyal Placeman's breast,
> Ere rude *Inquiry* broke his golden rest;
> Or cold Commissioners consign'd to fame,
> In rude Reports, the much-wrong'd Jobber's name—
> Ere Orange Squires were seen, with rueful faces,
> Round Frankland Lewis, crying "Spare our places;"
> And Loyalty might yet her votaries solace
> With funds, uncheck'd by honesty or Wallace!

The desperate habits of profusion, into which our gentry were
seduced, by this lottery of pensions and places at which all tried
their chance, were naturally followed by a considerable degree of
pecuniary embarrassment, which, like the cause that produced it,
soon affected all ranks. That race of little Protestant gentry,—between
whom and the Catholic slave the Penal laws had left a chasm, which
is not even yet filled up—had joined in this career of place-hunt-
ing and extravagance; and rents were raised, and money was bor-
rowed, to sustain it. Judgments, and Mortgages, and all those
other spectral things of the Law, that hover around the ruins of de-
cayed property, were now seen flitting in all directions; and it is
asserted that from about the year 1790, more lands have been sold
under decrees, than had been for the preceding hundred years.

It will not require much ingenuity to show, how favourable such
a state of things was to the general views of the Rock family. Often
have I lamented that my good old father did not live to see the
rapid fulfilment of his predictions, nor witness, at least, the beginning of that splendid career, which his son has now, for near forty
years, with but little interruption, triumphantly pursued.

The exorbitant rise of rents and the severe exaction of tithes[1],
were the grievances that, in the year 1787, drove the wretched
peasantry of Munster to my banners.

Lord Clare, who was then Attorney general, and, of course,
defended the Church, said, " he *knew* the unhappy tenantry were
ground to powder by relentless landlords." — Mr. Grattan, on the
other hand, proved that " the landlord's over-reaching, compared
to that of the tithe-farmer, was mercy." No wonder, therefore, that,
between both, the wretched people were maddened, to the full pitch
that Captain RIGHT (as I was then nick-named by my followers) required—not that even those double scourges, middlemen and tithe-
takers, efficient as they were, could have accomplished the object
for me so completely, had not the Government, as usual, come
in to their assistance, and by its premature and unqualified severity,
exasperated discontent into frenzy.

    * * * * * * * * * * * * * * *
            * * * * * *

The constancy of our State Doctors to their old remedy, the
bayonet, is miraculous. Having *exhibited* it in 1787 with their
accustomed vigour and success, they continued so to administer it,
at convenient intervals and with increasing exacerbation, till 1798
—when it brought on that violent, but imperfect, crisis, the Rebellion. They then resumed the same course of physic immediately
after the Union, and have persevered in it, only with a greater fre-
quency of doses, down to the present day—Martial Law and the
Insurrection Act having been in force fourteen years out of the
four and twenty that have elapsed since that measure. It would take
a whole page to enumerate the various forms and names, under
which this one, sole specific for all the evils of Ireland has been
administered, viz. Peace Preservation Acts, Seizure of Arms Act,
Secret Society Acts, Constabulary Acts, etc. etc. etc. etc. etc. But,
as Doctor Ollapod says, " Rhubarb is Rhubarb, call it what you
will; " and there is no disguising by any change of name or phrase,
that the bayonet is the sole, active ingredient in all these various
formulas.

When Molière was asked by Louis XIV. what use he made of his

---

[1] Mr. Grattan mentions an instance of a living in the disturbed districts, at this
time, being raised rapidly from 130*l.* a-year to 340*l*; and another, in the same
manner, being increased from 300*l.* to 1,000*l.*

[2] The Captain has here, in the original manuscript, entered into a long detail
of his achievements at this period, under the assumed name of Captain RIGHT:
but, as there is but little variety in his manner of relating these feats, and the
public has long been acquainted with the nature of them, I have thought it best to
omit the narration altogether.—EDITOR.

physician, he answered— "Nous causons ensemble; *il m'ordonne des remèdes — je ne les prends pas, et je guéris;*"—but, when a mischievous physician, who orders *steel* in all cases, has the power also of compelling his dose to be swallowed, what is the unfortunate patient to do?

CHAPTER X.

Conversation between the Captain and a Spirit.—Tithe systems in England and Ireland.—Differences between them.—Potatoes.—Tithe-farmers.—Proctors.—Ariosto.—Drivers —Scale of the Irish Hierarchy.—Paying Tithe in kind.—Siubad in the Valley of Diamonds.—New Tithe Bill.—Remarks on it.

IF a Spirit on his travels, like Micromegas, were to apply to me for information concerning this part of our planet, and I should tell him—"There is a class of men among us, set apart to instruct the people in religion, and to place before their eyes examples of piety and peacefulness. In order to qualify them for this mission, and give them, in their respective neighbourhoods, that popularity which is necessary to ensure its success, the Law empowers them to seize annually a tenth part of the produce of all the cultivators, however indigent, entrusted to their care.

"As this annual depredation is seldom taken in good part, and sometimes even leads to bloodshed and rebellion, the time of the said teachers is almost exclusively occupied, in wrangling with their pupils [1], and, occasionally, having them shot and hanged—in con-

---

[1] From a note on a speech of Sir Henry Parnell, in Cobbett's Parliamentary Debates, it appears that, in the year 1807, there were in five counties in Ireland no less than 1286 actions on cases connected with tithes; and in the Galway Advertiser of the 18th of October, 1822, we find the following article:—"At the quarter-sessions at Gort, one tithe-proctor processed eleven hundred persons for tithes. They were all, or most, of the lower order of farmers or peasants:—the expense of each process about eight shillings."

Anthony Pearson, in speaking of the law proceedings with respect to tithes, under the Protectorate, says, "Divers on this account have long lain in the Fleet, and yet are there. And I believe above an hundred suits are in the Exchequer depending, and proceedings stopt at this point, the very officers of the court relenting with pity towards such numbers of poor men, brought thither every term from the most remote parts of the nation, and some of them not for above twelvepence; such merciless cruelty lodges in the hearts of many, if not of most, of our pretended Gospel-ministers."

Milton, too, in speaking of the same reverend tithe-takers, says, "I omit their violent and irreligious exactions, their seizing of pots and pans from *the poor, who have as good a right to tithes as they,* from some the very beds; their seizing and imprisoning, worse than when the Canon Law was in force; worse than when the wicked sons of Eli were priests. For those sons of Belial, within some limits, made seizure of what they knew was their own by an undoubted law; but these,

sequence of which, they have but little leisure left for lessons of religion, and still less for examples of moderation and Christian charity.

" We have large law-books filled with cases, arising out of these amiable relations between the teachers and the taught. Yet, so fond are the former of this particular sort of wages of instruction, that they not only try to extract it from every thing they can lay their hands on [1], but declare daily, monthly, and quarterly, in news-papers, pamphlets, and reviews, that they prefer it to all other modes of getting money, that the wit of legislators or philosophers can devise.

" When questioned as to their reasons for this singular prefer-ence, they sometimes say, that it is on account of a certain reve-lation to Adam, the particulars of which have not transpired—at other times, they tell you, that Apollo and Hercules took the tenth of people's property, and, therefore, so must they—but the reason most generally and confidently given by them, is, that as teachers of religion, some hundred years since, shared this portion with the poor, the stranger, and the fatherless, they have now an undoubted and even sacred right to appropriate the whole of it exclusively to themselves."

If I were to state this to the Spirit, would he not stare?—and, if he were a Spirit, after Micromegas's own heart, would he not laugh?

Obnoxious and oppressive as Tithes have always been considered in England, there are reasons, manifest at the first glance, why they should be, beyond comparison, a more odious infliction in Ireland.

In England [2], where even abuses are forced to take a natural di-rection, tithes are paid to an Establishment in which the great majo-rity of the people have a direct interest—while in Ireland, from that unnatural position in which her Protestant Establishment places her,

from whom there is no sanctuary, seize out of men's ground, out of men's houses, their other goods, of double, sometimes of treble value, for that which, did not covetousness and rapine blind them, they know to be not their own by the Gospel which they preach."—*Considerations touching the likeliest means to remove Hirelings out of the Church.*

[1] "The Clergy," says Lord Holt, make every thing titheable; "but," he adds, "I do not regard that—the Pope, from whom they derive their claim, though they depart from its alleged application, subjected to tithe the gains of the mer-chant, and the pay of the army : the Canons went further, and held the tithe of fornication and adultery to be the undoubted property of the Church."

Sir Simon Degge, in his Chapter " Of what things Tithes shall not be paid," says, " No tithes shall be payable for hounds, *apes, popinjays, et similia.*"

[2] Some of these points of difference between English and Irish tithes, are put strongly in an excellent article upon the State of Ireland, in the Inquirer—for which, I suspect, we are indebted to the pen of that enlightened and patriotic member of parliament, Mr. Spring Rice.

thirteen-fourteenths of the people are thus taxed for the instruction of the small remaining fraction. Thus, to all the ill-blood that this exaction ever engendered in England, between a pastor and flock of the same religion, is added that deep hostility with which the members of a persecuted faith must ever regard those who have been their bitterest political enemies, and whom they are thus compelled to subsidize for trampling them to the earth.

" He who feedeth a flock (as our Reverend tithe-takers never cease telling us) hath a right to eat of the milk of the flock "— but in Ireland, where divine laws as well as human are reversed, it is from a flock which he does *not* feed, that the unconscionable shepherd extorts his milk.

When we consider, too, that this proscribed and fleeced race have also their own ministry to support, and that the poor peasant, placed between two Churches—the one his Good, the other his Evil Genius—is made tributary to both, for his misery [1] as well as his consolation, and with a blessing to the one, and a curse to the other, starves between them—*can* we expect any thing but discord and hate, from a system whose foundations lie so deep in anomaly and injustice, [2]— or can any modification or composition render innoxious, an inversion so monstrous of all the laws of reason and of nature?

Beside this radical difference in the very principle of the tax, as applied to the people of England and Ireland, there are others which contribute to render the mode of its operation and enforcement incomparably more odious and intolerable in the latter country.

[1] " Forced consecrations out of another man's estate are no better than forced vows, hateful to God who loves a *cheerful giver ; but much more hateful wrung out of men's purses to maintain a disapproved ministry* against their conscience; however unholy, infamous, and dishonourable to his ministers, and the free Gospel, maintained in such unworthy manner, by violence and extortion."— *Milton on Tithes.*

[2] English legislators can be wise enough every where but in Ireland. In Canada, for instance, Mr. Weld tells us, " Every religion is tolerated in the fullest sense of the word, and no disqualifications are imposed on any persons on account of their religious opinions. The Roman Catholic religion is that of the great majority of the inhabitants, and by the Quebec Bill of 1774, the ecclesiastics of that persuasion are empowered by law to recover all the dues which, previous to that period, they were accustomed to receive, as well as tithes—that is, from the Roman Catholic inhabitants ; *but they cannot exact any tithes, or dues, from Protestants, or of lands held by Protestants,* although formerly such lands might have been subjected to dues and tithes, for the support of the Roman Catholic church."

However absurd some of the old ecclesiastical Canons may be considered, it would have been well if the following principle laid down by the Canonists of the 11th and 12th century, had been consulted with respect to Ireland—" It is expressly held against the divine law, to convey tithes to any other church than where the owner commonly receives his soul's food."—*Selden.*

In England, the burthen is equally distributed among the farming classes—while in Ireland, where there is no Agistment tithe, it rests almost exclusively upon the lowest orders. In a Tithe-book, now lying before me, which I seized some time since among the baggage of a defeated Proctor, I find three gentlemen, holding fifteen hundred acres of the best land in the parish, charged for their tithe only four pounds among them; while a poor Catholic farmer in the neighbourhood, cultivating twenty acres of tillage, is made to pay for his corn and flax eight pounds—being twice as much towards the support of the Protestant Church as these three Protestant gentlemen contribute all together. There is, indeed, nothing more common than to see the rich grazier paying almost nothing to his own Clergyman, while the poor Catholic in his neighbour-hood, who raises (we will say) five acres of corn, three for the market and two for his own support, is obliged, out of this pittance, to pay the Clergymen of both modes of worship [1].

But there is still a more cruel exaction. The potatoe, the sole sustenance of the wretched peasantry of the South, is also pressed into the service of the Church—and there is not a parson in that part of the country, who does not live by the starvation of others. [2] Imagination, indeed, can hardly bring together a more incongruous compound, than the lofty Churchman, at one moment exalting his brow in spiritual authority, and, at the next, stooping to ransack the potatoe-pit of the cottager:

Quantum vertice ad auras
AEtherias, tantum *radice* in Tartara tendit.—VIRGIL.

We have here, too, another instance of the different point of view, in which the Clergy regard their own prescriptive rights and

[1] See "Letter from the Right Honourable Denis Brown, on the State of Ireland."—p. 11.

[2] Mr. Grattan mentions several instances, in the South of Ireland, of enormous charges made for tithes in years of famine, and pours out, justly, the whole thunder of his indignation against the Clergyman, who thus "takes advantage of a famine—brings up, as it were, the rear of divine vengeance, and becomes, in his own person, the last great scourge of the husbandman."
From a speech made by a Protestant gentleman, Mr. Colles, at one of the late Tithe meetings, it would appear that examples of such inhumanity are not infrequent. "In 1816," he said, "they could not but recollect, that one half of the crop was completely destroyed, by the heavy rains which fell incessantly during the harvest season, and the other half so materially damaged, as really to injure life while it seemed to sustain it. At that unexampled period of public calamity, when their fellow-creatures were perishing every where around them with hunger and disease, did the tithe-owners, from humanity at least, if not from justice, reduce their impositions, in proportion to the injury sustained by the crops? No —far from abating one jot of either the rate or rigour of their exactions, they levied their usual charges with their usual severity."

those of others. I have already shown, with what invincible steadi-
ness (though so ready to set aside any *modus* in favour of others)
they continue to profit by their own miserable *modus* of First-
fruits. And, here, in the instance of the potatoe-tithe,—indignant
as their Reverences have always been at the least innovation upon
their own ancient rights—we find them quietly taking possession
of an article, which neither law nor old usage recognizes as titheable,[1] and establishing, by means of their own tribunals, a claim
to it through the greater part of the South of Ireland.

Accordingly, in that potatoe-tithed region, have I always fixed
my head-quarters of Rebellion; and if, by good luck, the encroach-
ing spirit of the Church—which, modern as the introduction of
the potatoe is, has contrived thus effectually to "mark it for her
own"—should succeed in extending this tithe into the other provinces, the parsons and I shall, at length, like Jove and Cæsar, divide the empire of the whole island between us.

The employment of tithe-farmers and proctors is another part
of the machinery of this tax, from which England, luckily for the
repose of her farmers, is exempt[2]. Surveyors of tithes, indeed,
have been introduced into that country of late years; but if they
deserve the "lamentable" character given of them by Dr. Cove,
they must differ essentially from Irish valuators—"they have been
lamentably found (he says) by their employers to be at all times
disposed to favour the tithe-payers." In Ireland, however, by dint
of poundage fees and patronage, Dr. Cove's brethren manage to
render valuators much more orthodox.

Among us, the Tithe farmer is a sort of convenient step, by which
livings are enabled to mount in value, without any very violent
effort on the part of their possessors. For instance, an Incumbent
farms his tithes to some neighbour, who, by a skilful application
of that mechanic power called the Screw, increases the receipts sufficiently to afford an income for himself as well as the Parson. The
next Incumbent claims as his due the whole amount received by
this Tithe-farmer, and, in his turn, employs another Professor of

---

[1] In the same manner the Clergy of Ireland, at one time, illegally demanded
tithe for turf. "I have two decrees," said Mr. Grattan, "in my hand, from the
vicarial court of Cloyne;.the first excommunicating one man, the second excommunicating four men, most illegally, most arbitrarily, for refusing to pay tithe of
turf."

[2] Not wholly, however. In one of the Devon Agricultural Reports, we read,
—"In no part of England can the question of tithes be agitated with a less colour-
able pretext, than generally in the County of Devon. Some few instances of
tyranny and extortion have occurred within this district, but these were occa-
sioned by the tithe-proctors, or other persons renting the great tithes from the
church of Exeter."

9

the art of Screwing, who contrives, by the same process, to raise
the value of the living still higher, and transmits it, thus improved,
to the Incumbent who follows. So on, the mountain of oppression
is heaped up, while those prostrate Giants, the People, groan and
heave beneath it.

Of the Tithe-proctor I would willingly speak as becomes a generous enemy, in consideration of the many hard-fought fields in which
we have met together; and, without comparing his humbler efforts in the cause of Discord to those of his superiors—of an Archbishop, or even a Chancellor—I must say, that, in all the minor
requisites for teasing and goading a people, he performs his part
in a manner worthy of the system to which he belongs. The harassing assiduity with which he hovers round the crop—the perverseness with which he conceals the amount of his demand, lest the
farmer, apprised of its enormity, should proffer the tithe in kind—
his promptitude at a Citation, and his delight at a Distress, all are
perfect in their kind, and would turn Job himself into a Rockite.

Ariosto, in describing Discord, whom the angel Michael finds
in a church, where he had gone, in vain, to look for Silence, thus
equips her :—

> Di citatorie piene, e di libelle,
> D'esamini, e di carte di procure
> Havea le mani, e il sen, e gran fastelli
> Di chiose, di consigli, e di letture;
> Per cui le facultà de' poverelli
> Non sono mai nella città sicure.— Cant. 14.

that is (as Ariosto might describe the same Church personage in Ireland)—

> And Discord had her hands and bosom full
> Of Tithe citations, Proctors' bills, Distresses,—
> Libels, red-hot from mad————'s scull,—
> Pert Charges of Archbishops—pamphlets dull
> By Reverend F. T. C. D. A. double S's—
> And all the various boons the Church dispenses,
> To drive us, paupers, out of our seven senses! [1]

After the Proctor, the next link in this ecclesiastical chain—and

---

[1] The following more faithful version is from the forthcoming Cantos of
Mr. W. Rose's spirited Translation.

> Examinations, summonses, and store
> Of writs and letters of attorney, she
> In both her hands, and in her bosom bore,
> And acts and deeds, the law's artillery:
> Against which arms the substance of the poor
> Can never safe in walled city be.
> Before, behind her, and about her wait
> Attorney, notary, and advocate.

the lowest, if the hangman does not claim that place—is the Driver. The office of this personage is (under the decree of a Court,[1] where Tithe owners are the judges, and where a Citation for a tithe of 18s. 10d. cost defendant 2l. 10s.)[2] to drive away the cattle of the insolvent farmer, or—as in the Rev. Mr. Morrit's case—to " distrain five sheep for a tithe of five shillings, and buy them himself, under the distress, for a shilling each afterwards."

The ascent from these minor agents of the Irish hierarchy, up through the gradations of curate, vicar, rector, etc. into the loftiest regions of Episcopacy and Primacy, resembles that Scale of Being, which Locke supposes to exist in the Universe, ascending gradually from the lowest to the sublimest and most etherialized essences; and, between the two extremes—the Driver, who for the good of

[1] See for a statement of the exactions of those Courts, and of the iniquities of the Tithe system in general throughout Ireland, a Pamphlet just published, entitled, " A Report of the Committee of the Parish of Blackrath, in the county of Kilkenny." The following is a specimen of the expenses to which a poor man is put by a Citation to the Bishop's Court: " The whole sum in dispute is 6s.; the fee to counsel is a guinea. The very first step, therefore, that the poor man takes for his defence, he has to pay nearly four times the amount of the demand that he contests. He has next to pay two Citations for his two witnesses 13s. 6d.—that is to say, 12s. 6d. for the first, and 1s. for the second." The trial generally ends in a decree against the unfortunate peasant, which is followed up by a monition—and the costs of both are stated to add near 2l. 16s. 8d. to his losses. He is then handed over to the secular arm; " The parson processes his wretched parishioner to the Civil-bill Court : there he is decreed, as a matter of course, without being even allowed (strange to say!) to enter into the merits of his case. And what costs follow? The costs of the decree are 1s. 11d.; the costs of the warrant 1s. 1d.; the fees of the Bailiff who executes the warrants are 2s. 4d.; the fees of the two keepers who watch the distress for four days and nights amount (at 2s, 6d. a day for each) to 1l.; and lastly, the Auctioneer's fees come to 6s. 3d. making altogether the sum of 6l. 12s. 2d., so that the Clergyman sells the whole crop to satisfy the Tithes, and turns the miserable wretch, his wife and children, to the road, to beg or to steal, or to starve. High-spirited as the poor Irishman may be, he will never have the courage to renew the contest against such powerful odds."

[2] So stated by Sir Henry Parnell, July 5, 1820. I have given this more moderate estimate in order to be on the safe side, though convinced, myself, that the Pamphlet quoted in the preceding note has not over-stated the enormity of these proceedings.

See, for an account of the tyranny and extortion of these Ecclesiastical Courts, Mr. Grattan's admirable Speech on Tithes—one of the few specimens of parliamentary eloquence, that deserve to be placed beside the great master-pieces of Burke.

A Reverend pamphleteer, whom I have more than once quoted, ("Case of the Church of Ireland stated") has had the good taste and feeling to refer to the glorious era of our great Patriot's fame, as "the loquacious days of Mr. Grattan!" This is quite worthy of the University, to which, I understand, the Reverend writer belongs—and which once expressed its feeling towards the same illustrious man, in an equally dignified and tasteful manner, by turning his picture in one of the public Halls upside down!

the Church, puts the Catholic's cow *into* the pound, and the Prelate who, for the same pious purpose, keeps the Catholic himself *out of* the Constitution—there is a sympathy of sentiment and unity of design, which is felt through all the intermediate range, and, like the sensitiveness of the spider, "lives along the line."

Of the detestation in which the payment of tithes is held, independently of its pressure as a heavy and unequal tax, we cannot require a more convincing proof, than is furnished by a fact which Lord Maryborough mentioned, on the occasion of Sir Henry Parnell's motion on the subject of Tithes. "I asked," says his Lordship, "an Honourable friend of mine this morning, a part of whose estate is tithe-free, what was the difference of the rent which he received for his land that was tithe-free, and that which was not? He told me he received ten shillings an acre more for the land that was tithe-free than he did for the other. I then asked him, what was the amount of the tithe on that part of his land of equal quality and contiguous to the other, which was subject to it? He said about fourteen-pence an acre!"

From this we perceive, so odious is the nature of this tax, that without any other difference between the two parts of the land, than that one was exempt from the harassing visitation of the Tithe-proctor, ten shillings more was given for this precious immunity alone—or, in other words, that the farmer willingly paid 8s. 10d. in the form of rent, to escape 1s. 2d. in the hateful form of tithe. This sample alone, though quoted by Lord Maryborough and the Bishop of Ferns for a very different purpose, speaks volumes as to the feeling of repugnance with which this "Therumah of an evil eye" is regarded.

There is yet another strong proof of the hardship and disgust which the present mode of paying these dues produces. The practice of setting out the tithe in kind, which in England is considered a grievance by the farmers, and accordingly very seldom adopted[1], would, among us, be hailed as a most welcome relief[2] from all the worrying process of valuations, citations, promissory notes, etc.

---

[1] In looking through the County Reports of England, we find the instances of tithe taken in kind but rare. Thus, in one of the Bedford Agricultural Reports— 'From minute investigation, not one rector in ten takes his tithe in kind, and I heard of only one or two vicars who did so—and probably they were driven to this measure by the stubborn opposition of their parishioners."

[2] Among the late efforts at composition, under the new Tithe Bill, there is an instance of a Rev. Gentleman who having refused 1,200l. a year, as being an inadequate compensation for his tithes, was required by his parishioners, in consequence, to receive the payment of them in kind—but this he also refused, and politely answered all the notices he received, by citations to the Bishop's Court.

to which the mode of composition under the auspices of the proctor leads — and to be allowed the free exercise of this right of paying in kind (which, though the laws permits, the Ecclesiastical Courts obstruct and frustrate) [1] is, at present—next to the supreme bliss of not paying any such tax at all—the chief ambition of the great majority of tithe-payers.

Combination in serving notices is what the Parson dreads—and the Parson, I own, is fully justified in dreading every possible inconvenience that this affectionate flock can inflict on him.[2] Wealthy as most of these Reverend persons are, there is no denying that they earn their opulence dearly. They are like Sinbad in the Valley of Diamonds—walking amidst wealth, but not at all comfortable. I have myself seen the Archbishop of Cashel [3] taking his morning drive protected by a large escort of dragoons; and I could name more than one worthy Rector, whose pistols are, at least, as necessary a companion of his walks as his prayerbook.

On this very subject of setting out the tithe in kind, such a charitable feeling is there abroad towards the Church, that some persons of considerable legal acuteness have taken the trouble of drawing up a code of instructions for the peasantry [4], by which they may, without disturbing a single curl of the Law, combine against the Parson, "sans que cela paraisse,"—and make the collection of tithes in this way almost as harassing to *him*, as his own favourite mode of enforcing it has always been to *them*.

With respect to the new Tithe Bill of Mr. Goulburn, which is at present running the gauntlet through the vestries of the South, I confess I do not apprehend much danger to the ROCK interest from its success. Its first and obvious effect is, to increase the

[1] Frequently, too, when the poor man sets out his tithe in kind, "the Clergy first suffer the tenth of the crop to rot on the ground, and then recover the amount of it in their own Court—thus compelling the peasant to pay the same tithes twice over; once in kind, and again in money."—*Statement relative to the Bishop's Court.*

[2] A specimen of the way in which a spiritual teacher may be annoyed by his pupils, in drawing the tithe in kind, is found in an Agricultural Report of the County of Hants. The farmer gave the Clergyman notice, that he was going to draw a field of turnips on a certain day. The clergyman accordingly sent his team and servant at the time appointed, when the former drew ten turnips and desired the other to take one of them—saying he would not draw any more that day, but would let him know when he did.

[3] Not the present Archbishop—no—reprobate as I am, I can still admire candour, liberality, and humanity; and to such Churchmen as Lawrence, Jebb, and the late Archbishop of Tuam, I am ready to give a Safe-conduct through my realms at any time.

[4] See some very clever Letters to this effect, which appeared last Summer, in the Southern Reporter, and which well deserve to be collected.

wealth and power of the Church—which is, as Shakespeare says,

To guard a title that was rich before,
To gild refined gold and paint the (orange) lily.

To say nothing of the tender care that has been shown for the interests of the Clergy, by taking, as a standard of composition, the average of the most high-priced years—that rich Agistment Tithe, of which they were deprived in 1735, and which abridged their incomes, it was supposed, by one fifth, will, by this act, if put in force, be virtually restored to them. Thus, that Paradise [1] of fair demesnes and lawns, from which the "flaming brand" of the Irish Parliament chased them—those

fields, beloved in vain,
Where once the cureless priesthood stray'd,

and for the loss of which neither the fruits of increasing tillage, nor the Unions of many Parishes, nor the grants of many parliaments, have been able to console them, will, under the kindly auspices of Mr. Goulburn, again be enjoyed.

The additional powers given to the Parson by this Act are also considerable. In the first place, the owner of the soil, if not a farmer himself, is excluded from all interference in the disposal of his own property, and the Incumbent and his parishioners are left to settle the whole matter between them. In the next place, the parson is authorised, for the recovery of his tithe, to distrain, and exercise all the other powers actually exercised by a landlord for the recovery of his rent. In the third place, the precedence given to tithes over all other claims, of rent, family incumbrances, etc. etc. leaves to the landlord, whose tenant has been a defaulter under the composition, only the gleanings of the parson's Distress to satisfy his demand for rent. Such are a few of the features of this

· [1] The deep feeling with which the loss of this Tithe is remembered, at a distance of nearly eighty years, may be judged from the pathetic and indignant terms in which the Right Reverend author of a late pamphlet alludes to it. "If a tyrannical power has repelled the clergyman from the rich and extensive demesnes, which should have contributed largely to his income, etc. etc."—Appendix to a Second Edition of an "Inquiry," etc.

The mis representations in this Appendix with respect to Lay Impropriators, are such as might be expected from the candour of a writer, who thinks Adam Smith a bad authority on the subject of tithes, because he was the friend of Hume! —Far from wishing to "separate the cases of the Lay Impropriator and the Clergyman," the Duke of Devonshire, in presenting the petition from the Corporation of Waterford in 1822, expressed his readiness, as an Impropriator of more than 20 parishes, to make every sacrifice on his part for a satisfactory arrangement of tithes. Lord Lansdowne has frequently made the same declaration; and few, I think, will join the Right Reverend writer, in questioning the sincerity of these two noble persons.

bill, by which our sagacious rulers propose to moderate the exactions
of the Church, and put an end to the dissatisfaction of tithe-payers.

Though but little inclined to pity our Landed Gentry, for any
sacrifices they may be forced to make to their starving tenantry, I
cannot but confess that the encroachments of this measure on their
property are such as to give very reasonable grounds of complaint.
Selfish and unprincipled as was the vote of 1735, by which the
Commons of Ireland transferred the burthen of tithe from their own
rich pastures and demesnes to the conacre and potatoe-garden of the
cottager, it was yet confirmed and made a law of the land by the
Act of Union. Its confirmation was, indeed, one among the many
foul bribes, out of which that unnatural measure arose—like Frank-
enstein's ghastly patch-work, made up of contributions from the
whole charnel-house of political corruption.

Under the security of this arrangement, many who did not share
in its infamy, have since taken and let farms, bought and sold
lands—without a view to the possibility of any future conjuror, like
Mr. Goulburn, again evoking the spirit of the Agistment tithe out
of that " vasty deep," in which, with Ireland's independence, it
seemed to have been laid asleep for ever. Yet now, after a lapse of
four-and-twenty years, forth comes the Secretary, holding the
Parson by the hand, and, reopening to him, in generous contempt
of the law, all those " fresh fields and pastures new " which the
Act of Union had pronouced to be sacred from him for ever, exclaims

> I nunc, magnificos victor molire-triumphos,
> Cinge comam lauro ; votaque redde jovi.

> Go now, in triumph tread the Squire's domains,
> And thank the Gods and Goulburn for thy gains.

Thus it is that one injustice generates another, and that the breed
is propagated, with more than leporine fecundity, through every
successive measure, which these third-rate Legislators, these Statesmen *in waiting*, are sent to inflict upon Ireland.

If the poor tenantry were likely to profit by this infraction of
justice towards the landlord—if the advantage that ought to arise to
the small cultivator, from a more equal distribution of the burthen
which now falls exclusively upon him, were really and practically
to accrue from this measure—I should say, " do wrong," for once,
" with a right cause "—break as many Articles of the Union as you
please—invest the parson with a tenth of the fee of every estate in
Ireland—do any thing, so you lighten the load of misery which at
present weighs down the peasantry to the very earth.

But the fact is, the great increase of the general amount of tithe

which this Act must produce—together with the summary powers
given to the parson for the enforcement of his full demand—will
render the pressure of the tax intolerable to the extensive farmer,
from whom the miserable cottiers hold their small spots of land;
and it will only be by raising the rents on the latter,—if, indeed, the
back of misery can bear any addition without breaking—he can
hope to meet the increased demands upon his means, or to his
property out of the fangs of that law harpy, Distress. Thus, the
trifling advantage gained in one quarter (for to the small farmer of
from 5 to 20 acres the Bill may bring some relief) is more than coun-
terbalanced by increased misery in another.

The potatoe-garden, too, that last boundary between the peasant
and famine—which, every where, but in the South, is still kept
sacred from the Clergy—will, by the applotments under this Act,
wherever they exist, be swept into one general mass of contribution,
towards the further enrichment of the Protestant Church of Ireland.

I have here spoken of this measure, as any lover of *tranquillity*
might, who wished to see some more rational remedy for the discontent that reigns among us. But, speaking in my own person as
CAPTAIN ROCK, I must say that, though perfectly satisfied with the
results of the old system, I am equally ready to try this, or any
other new strain of discord, which may be struck up for us by our
State musicians—whose ideas of a concert, especially among themselves, seem to have been founded upon that famous *charivari* of
Rousseau at Lausanne, in which no two instruments were upon the
same scent.

It will be perceived that the capabilities of the Bill for all purposes
of discontent are infinite. Indeed, the Clergy are, at present, the
only class of persons satisfied with it—though, on the first announcement of the intended innovation, their alarm for the "silver shrines"
of their Great Diana was so strong, as even to bring forth an address
from the Archbishops and Bishops, declaring that the measure
"would be unquestionably destructive of the independence of the
Church Establishment, and, in their judgment, equally destructive
of its respectability, its utility, and its permanence."

This was a pretty strong declaration of the clerical feeling on the
subject, and it was thought that a compulsory clause would be necessary—a sort of "douce violence"—to compel these reverend
persons to avail themselves of the Act. As soon, however, as they
found out, from a nearer acquaintance with the measure, that, so far
from injuring their silver Diana in the least, its object was to make
her even more silver than before, their clamours against the bill
were at once turned into activity *for* it—they were the first to apply
to the Lord Lieutenant for powers to act under it, and they have

been the life and soul of all its movements through the vestries ever since—claiming, of course, in most cases, the full average, and expressing their regret that, under the Act, they were not " at liberty" to take less.

How far such open and officious zeal for the measure is decently reconcileable with the opinion expressed of it by the Prelates, it is not for me to inquire. But, prompt as the clergy have thus naturally shown themselves, to take advantage of all the worldly benefits of the Bill, I rather think that in their hearts they agree with the Archbishops and Bishops ; and will not easily forgive the profanation which the Tabernacle has suffered, in being touched, even for the sake of enriching it, by the unholy hand of the Law. It is said of a certain King that, on being once saved from falling by the vigorous grasp of one of his attendants, he so far forgot the value of the service in the familiarity of the means, as to cry out pettishly, when restored to his equilibrium, " never touch a King "—and, in the same manner, I suspect, the Irish clergy will resent the violation, even while they profit by it. It is the first direct interference of the Legislature with the *jus divinum* of their property, and they naturally feel it may not be the last.

Hæ nugæ in seria ducent.

i. e. in English ,

The hand that touches Tithes may, when it suits , —
Prodigious boldness!—meddle with First Fruits !

CHAPTER XI.

1793—1796.

The Captain again alarmed by some symptoms of wisdom in the government—his fears proved to be groundless.—Montaigne's tailor.—Lord Fitzwilliam recalled.—Lord Camden appointed.—Concessions in 1793. Rendered of little avail by the Orange Ascendancy.—Map of the Moon. —Corporation spirit.—Catholic Emancipation.—The Captain's gratitude to his friends, Mr. Peel, Lord Eldon, etc., etc.

" As long as Millions shall kneel down
To ask of Thousands for their own,
While Thousands proudly turn away,
And to the Millions answer 'Nay !'
So long the merry reign shall be
Of CAPTAIN ROCK and his family !"

THIS important part of our family Prophecy (which cannot be too often before the eyes of the reader) seemed placed in some degree of jeopardy by the concessions to the Catholics in 1793 ; and, still more, by the hope of their complete emancipation, which, under the government of Lord Fitzwilliam, was awakened in all hearts—solely, it would seem, for the purpose of being wantonly extinguished again.

Notwithstanding my father's repeated warnings to me, never to let my confidence in the Rock cause be shaken by any momentary appearances of justice and liberality in the Government, I confess myself to have been one among the many who were at this period deceived—and who thought that it was, at last, really the intention of our rulers, to remove all the remaining fetters of the Catholics, and thus alienate to the Crown the allegiance of the great majority of my followers.

In the first place, I knew that if the peace and security of the country were objects at all likely to weigh, in the minds of such statesmen, against their old love of mis-government and their rooted passion for pains and penalties, there never was a moment when redress of grievances was more necessary—not only to satisfy the just claims of a great portion of the people, but to disperse the elements of a conspiracy then known to be forming, and professing to embrace in its circle all ranks and sects of Irishmen.

The Roman Catholics had, as yet, held off from this confederacy. The partial concessions of 1793, however ungraciously bestowed, had awakened a feeling of loyalty throughout that body—a feeling, born in gratitude, and kept alive by hope—which not even the seduction of those fair republican theories, then adopted with such enthusiasm by the Protestants and Presbyterians of the North, could weaken or disturb. The truth is, they had stood too long in the darkness of proscription, to bear at once so full an illumination of liberty, as their more daring and intelligent fellow countrymen would let in upon them; and preferred gradually feeling their own way into light, to the risks which a bolder struggle would incur, and which they had been too long slaves to have the hardihood to encounter.

Judging by the ordinary rules of common sense (which is a test, however, never to be applied to the administration of affairs in Ireland), it seemed to be a matter of the most vital importance to the State, to keep these humble aspirants for freedom still steady in the paths of loyalty—preventing them, by a prompt removal of their wrongs, from falling into the arms of those who were bidding high for their alliance, and to whose conspiracy their alliance was, indeed, an indispensable object, as alone furnishing that numerical and physical strength, without which their own plans of rebellion and revolution would have been mere dreams.

All these considerations appeared to me to make up such a strong case of self-interest on the side of justice, that—notwithstanding the old antipathy of our rulers to the latter quality—I thought it possible that a selfish regard for peace and their own safety would prevail, and that they were actually and truly about to make lasting friends of the Catholics.

But in this I was mistaken. " I have an honest lad for my tailor," says Montaigne, " whom I never knew guilty of a single truth— no, not even when it would have been to his advantage; " and just so has it ever been with the Irish Government—they have shown themselves incapable of performing an act of justice, even when it was decidedly and obviously for their advantage.

In order, too, to render the disappointment more galling to the Catholics—to treat them according to the eagle's mode of breaking the tortoise, and carry their hearts up high into the regions of hope, only that they might be dashed down more effectually after-wards—all the preliminaries of their Emancipation were gone through with the most imposing solemnity. The Duke of Portland had stipulated, on his coalescing with Mr. Pitt, for a complete change in the mode of governing Ireland '—which he pronounced (as he well might) to be " execrable," and full of danger, not only to Ireland, but to the empire itself. Lord Fitzwilliam, the political friend of Mr. Grattan, Mr. Ponsonby, and all those who had exerted themselves most strenuously for the entire Emancipation of the Catholics, was the person selected to carry the meditated reforms into effect. The Beresford faction, which, for years, had made a job of all Ireland, was threatened with dismissal. Grattan—the Diomede of the Catholic cause, upon whose helm the unwearied light ² of wisdom ever shone—was seen in the van of the new Administration. The Act of total Enfranchisement was already in progress—scarce a murmur of dissatisfaction was heard abroad, and even the accustomed croak of the Corporation was weak and solitary. —when, just at this moment of hope and triumph, while the great Drama of public pacification was proceeding happily to its close, the stage became suddenly darkened round the actors—the principal personage, Lord Fitzwilliam, was mysteriously spirited away from the scene ³, and the curtain fell on the hopes of the Catholics, if we may believe Mr. Peel, for ever!

' "When the Duke of Portland and his friends were to be enticed into a coalition with Mr. Pitt's administration, it was necessary to hold out such lures as would make the coalition palatable. If the general management and superintendence of Ireland had not been offered to his Grace, that coalition could never have taken place." *Letter from Lord Fitzwilliam to Lord Carlisle.*

² Ακαματον πυρ. Homer.

³ No liberal Lord Lieutenant has ever been suffered to remain long in Ireland. Sir Antony Bellingham was recalled, after the death of Henry 8th, "for not sufficiently oppressing the Irish." Sir John Perrot, in the reign of Elizabeth, was removed for the same reason; and of Lord Radnor, who was Lord Lieutenant in

In recounting such instances of gross and wanton perfidy, it is impossible even for *me* to feel otherwise than deeply serious. " The man ," says Cicero , " who could laugh on such occasions , is no true citizen."

It is needless to add what were the necessary consequences of this insulting mockery of a nation's claims and hopes. The Catholics carried their despair and their numbers into the ranks of the United Irishmen [1]—Lords Camden and Castlereagh took the places of Lord Fitzwilliam and Mr. Grattan, and the system of whipping, burning, and free-quarters began.

As the concessions of 1793 form the sum total of the liberty of the Catholics at present—notwithstanding the promises held out to them at the Union and broken as magnanimously as every other promise — let us see whether the liberality of the " Thousands " to the " Millions ," at that period, was such as to alarm CAPTAIN ROCK for the continuance of his " merry reign; " —always recollecting that those liberalities were brought forth in a moment of panic ; and that most of them have been since so checked and stunted by their unnatural parents, as to resemble the curse-stricken progeny of the countess of Hainault—numerous, but abortive, and mere *lusus naturæ* of legislation.

In the first place, with respect to the Elective Franchise : — By conceding the power of *electing ,* and withholding the right of *representing,* the Act of 1793 admitted all the worst part of the Catholic population into the Constitution, and kept the best out of it. Thus, as the Emperor Commodus was said to be mischievous even in his jests, the Legislature of Ireland has contrived to be pernicious even in its benefits. The forty-shilling freeholders are among the acknowledged curses of the country—being one of the chief causes of Common Leases, Joint Tenantcy [2], and all that endless subdivision of penury, which—to a degree almost to realize the " infinite parva" of the mathematicians—is carried on among us.

The Catholics themselves , more wise in their wants, suggested , in their application for relief in 1792 , the expediency of fixing a higher rate of qualification for them than for Protestant electors. But

the time of Charles and , Lord Orford says—" we are not told how he disappointed the King's expectations, probably not by too much complaisance, nor why his administration, which Burnet calls ' just,' was disliked. If it is true that he was a good governor, the presumption will be, that his rule was not disliked by those *to* whom but *from* whom he was sent."

[1] The united Irishmen (according to the memoir drawn up by Emmet) " used the recall of Lord Fitzwilliam and the rejection of his measures , to cement together in political union the Catholic and Protestant masses."

[2] This evil has been remedied by a late Bill.

the very same Parliament that then rejected their whole petition with scorn! in the very next year precipitately granted, in this one mischievous respect, more than they asked for; and while they still excluded from the senate the few Catholics that could *serve* the country, let in upon the hustings the whole mob they had themselves brutalized, to ruin it;—like that judicious emancipator, Don Quixote, when he liberated the galley slaves, and found it no easy matter to defend himself against them afterwards.

Nor let it be forgotten, in our account of gratitude with the Government, that this grant of the Elective Franchise to the Catholics would soon have become a matter of necessity, even if panic had not extorted the concession then. Already had the great decrease of the Protestant population given warning that a day was not far distant, when, if Catholics were not admitted to this Franchise, the same cause, that now threatens to leave the Protestant Church without a Laity, would have left the protestant Parliament without Electors. In vain had the Legislature tried, at different periods, to import Protestant electors from Germany, Geneva, etc.; and endeavoured even, as we have seen, to prevail upon Jews, to come and assist in making Representatives of the people of Ireland. These statesmanlike plans had all failed; and it would have been found necessary, even for the mere carrying on of the farce of representation, to drive herds of Catholic serfs into the vote-market at last.

The Freedom of Corporations is one of those rights, which the statute of 1793 restored to the Catholics, but which the spirit of Orangeism frustrates and almost wholly nullifies. The astronomer Ricciolus, in his Map of the Moon, kindly marked out certain portions of land in that planet, as estates for some of his brother astronomers—and about as nominal and unreal as those Lunar properties, are most of the privileges acceded by the existing law to the Catholics.

With respect to the Freedom of Corporations,—the long exclusion of Catholics from the exercise of this right having, in general, deprived them of the two chief claims to it, Birth and Service, they have no other mode left of acquiring their freedom but by Special Grant—and this their Protestant masters take special care not to indulge them with. The few Catholic Freemen in the Guilds of Dublin (stated, in 1812, to be not a hundred out of the 2,400 of which those Guilds consist) are excluded by the Corporation at large from the right of voting at elections of Members for the City—so that the Elective Franchise in such cases becomes a mere nullity, and the laws themselves are rendered useless—by the Faction which thus sets itself above them.

The same evil principle of Orangeism and Intolerance pervades

all the Corporate Towns in Ireland—which may be reckoned, if I
recollect right, at 115 in number—and when to this general operation of the *spirit* of the law against its *letter*, we add the actual enactments which exclude the Catholic from all Corporate Offices [1]—from
any share whatever in those municipal privileges and immunities,
which, unjust, partial, and exclusive as they are in their nature,
become aggravated, in their very worst features by being thus narrowed to a small favoured Sect—we may have some idea of the extent
to which the penal spirit spreads itself through Ireland, and how
universally it " comes home to men's business and bosoms," in the
most familiar, daily, and interesting concerns of their life.

Imagine one of these towns, where a small Orange Oligarchy,
combining all the petty jealousies of the Corporation spirit with
the arrogant prejudices of a dominant and long-privileged sect, en-
grosses to itself the sole management of all municipal affairs — the
impositions of various tolls and duties, from which themselves are
exempt—the monopoly of trades and arts by the system of legal ap-
prenticeships—the appointment to the numerous lucrative situations, dependant upon the Corporate Offices—in short, all those
branches of civic and parochial patronage, which go to make the
consequence and influence of such small municipal governments.

What must be the lot of Catholic farmer, merchant, or tradesman,
under the vexatious control of this little knot of bigoted burgesses?
Oppressed by partial levies—by excessive market-tolls—by invidious
preferences, which, while they obstruct Catholic industry, encourage and pamper up Protestant insolence—by all that grinding machinery of exaction and injustice, which has been laid open during
the late inquiry into the abuses of the Corporation of Limerick—is
it wonderful that the victim should hate and curse a system, which
thus meets him, at every turning of life, with its odious scowl of
exclusion, which, like the branding-iron, inflicts at once both suffering and disgrace, and which insults him by the very confidence
with which it presumes on his patience!—is it wonderful that
CAPTAIN ROCK should count upon a long and successful reign,
among a people thus taught to feel that the law is only powerful to
oppress; that the slightest infusion of justice or liberality into it pa-
ralyses its strength—and that, like Mithridates, from long habit, the
only food upon which it thrives is poison.

If long practice, indeed, in the art of governing wrongly, must

_____

[1] The number of Corporate Offices throughout Ireland, from which Catholics
are excluded by the express word of the law, is calculated to be no less than 3,548;
to these, if we add the situations, immediately dependant on them, from which
Catholics are by consequence equally excluded, it will make a total of near 5,000
Corporate Offices, to which this Penal interdict extends.

necessarily produce an incapacity of governing otherwise, our rulers have, at least, *this* excuse for the continuance of their injustice. " Allez, Monsieur"—says a personage in the *Malade Imaginaire*, to an apothecary, whose practice had only lain in the lowest ministry of his profession—" on voit bien que vous n'avez pas été accoutumé à parler à des visages ; " and, in like manner, the inveterate Faction that rules us, has so long communed only with the baser parts of legislation, that they can hardly be expected to know the face of Justice, even when they see it.

To return to the Act of 1793—Catholics were by this statute made eligible to serve on Grand and Petty Juries [1] : but, that as little utility as possible might be extracted from the privilege, the office of Sheriff, from which the appointment of the Juries flows, is still kept exclusively in the hands of the Protestants—thus leaving the Catholic's chance of ever appearing on those tribunals, at the mercy of the same "disinheriting countenance ," which frowns him out of his rights wherever it encounters him. Accordingly, there are some Counties where no Roman Catholic has ever been on a jury, when a person of his own religion was to be tried [2]—and it was mentioned by an Irish member of high authority, during the last session, that he had heard a leading gentleman of a County " thank God, that, for the space of 100 years, no Catholic had ever sat on the trial either of Protestant or Catholic in that jurisdiction."

It was, indeed, avowed, during the late inquiry into the conduct of the Sheriff of Dublin, that though, upon some unimportant occasions, Catholics are allowed to serve on the Grand Jury, yet, that, wherever their own rights are concerned, or their money to be disposed of, they are without ceremony excluded.

At the mysteries of the Bona Dea in ancient Rome, no male creature was allowed to be present; and it seems that the mysteries of Jobbing—the " nullis sacra retecta" of Peculation—are to be kept equally sacred from the profane eyes of Catholics. To what an extent these select Protestant Grand Juries used to carry their high

---

[1] They were already eligible—but under a restrictive Statute, enacted in 1708, the mere *letter* of which was repealed in 1793, while its spirit was still left in full force.

[2] Wakefield says, in speaking of Tipperary—" there are some large estates belonging to Catholics, and during the Duke of Bedford's administration, seven gentlemen of that persuasion were always called on the Grand Jury ; but, when I was there in 1808 and 1809, not one was called, the nomination of Sheriff being entirely an office of party." Of an other County he says, " During the Duke of Bedford's administration, three or four Catholics were on the Grand Jury. In 1808, and 1809 none were called; but I understood, that at the Spring Assizes of 1811, the Sheriff was favourably disposed towards them."

and peculiar privilege of fleecing the public [1], is well known to the
Legislature, which has, at last, interfered to check their enormities
—and how interested they were in turning religion to account, by
excluding all heterodox sharers of the spoil, may be judged from
a fact, lately stated by Lord Bathurst, that, at a time when the
revenue of Ireland amounted altogether to but four millions, one
million of that sum passed, unaccounted for, through the hands
of Grand Juries.

When Pericles told Alcibiades that he was considering how he
should be able to make up his accounts for the public assembly,
"rather," said Alcibiades, "consider how you may avoid giving
any accounts at all." If Alcibiades had served all his life upon Irish
Grand Juries and at Irish Public Boards, he could not have uttered
a more golden sentence on the subject of Jobbing than this.

Permission to enter into the Profession of the Law was another of
the privileges accorded in 1793 : and, as an opening of fame and
emolument to the Catholic—as an opportunity, too, of showing
that Nature, at least, is no sectarian, and that talents may be possessed without the intervention of a test-oath—the concession has
been attended with no inconsiderable advantage to him.

But here, as every where else, he is stopped in the propylæum
of the temple. He may raise his voice to ask for justice to his fellow
slaves, but from the inner shrine, where it is dispensed, he is
utterly excluded. He can neither be Judge, Attorney general,
King's counsel, master in Chancery, Recorder, nor any one of a
long list of near 200 offices, from all of which the express letter of
the Statutes excludes him. In addition to these, there are various
other legal situations—such as Commissioners of Bankrupts, Assis-
tant Barristers, etc., between which and him, though the laws
have left them open [2], the Ascendancy throws up its blank barrier
—separating him from all the honours and rewards of his profession, and marking him among the condemned of the land, even in
the very seat and asylum of justice.

The consequence is, that the people, against whom the law is
arrayed, cannot discover, in looking through its official ranks, one
single individual of their own faith, upon whom they can count for
a community of feeling, or for a chance of impartiality between
them and their accusers [3].

<hr/>

[1] Mr. Dutton, in his Survey of Clare, mentions, as a fact, that " a Grand juror
asked, and was actually paid 3ol, for using his influence in procuring a presentment."
[2] It has been calculated by Mr. Scully, that the number of Law Offices from
which the Catholic is excluded, both by express enactments, and the consequent
operation of these enactments, amounts altogether to about 1,500.
[3] "In this country (says Mr. Grattan) there are two codes of laws, one for the

Notwithstanding all this, it is often gravely asserted, that the question of Emancipation regards only the upper ranks of the Catholics, and that to the lower orders it is an object of but little importance or concern [1]! Go, you, who entertain this sagacious opinion—go ask the poor Catholic, who sees himself excluded from the Vestry, where a few Protestants vote away his wretched means of subsistence, to provide for the building and repairs of their own church—where, though forbidden to have a voice in the election of a Church-warden, he may be capriciously compelled to act as Church-warden himself [2] — ask the farmer, who is cited to the Bishop's court by a Reverend tithe-owner, and finds another Reverend tithe-owner on the Bench to decide between them [3]—ask the Catholic of the North, who, surrounded by armed Orangemen, is left wholly at their mercy by that Penal law, which forbids him to use arms for his self-defence [4]; who, if found with weapons, may be transported, if found without them, may be murdered—ask the Catholic inhabitants of towns and cities, whom the spirit of Corporation Ascendancy haunts through all the details of life; who

Protestant sect, another for the Catholic. The Legislature has a common interest with the one, and against the other. The Protestant beggar, therefore, has an advantage over the Catholic proprietor."

[1] Even the acute Author of "the Past and Present State of Ireland," asserts that, "expedient as Catholic Emancipation may be, it is *only* expedient."

[2] Thus reversing to the poor man the hardship of his betters, who may *elect*, but cannot *represent*.

The danger of this little system of parochial tyranny is evident. Where the office of Church-warden is attended with profit or patronage, the Protestants keep it to themselves; but where it brings only trouble or expense, the burthen may be thrown upon the Catholic.

[3] "Is it likely that a Clergyman, who must naturally feel a bias to the interests of the Clergy, as opposed to those of the laity, should be an *impartial judge*? Again, is it likely that a Tithe-owner, who holds Tithes in the very Diocese, should be a *disinterested judge*? And lastly, is it likely, that an humble Ecclesiastic depending altogether for preferment in the Church, on the absolute will of his Bishop, who might (as he well knows) be prejudiced against him by the Clergy, were he to venture to check their exactions, should be an *independent judge*?"—*Report of the Committee of the Parish of Blackrath.*

[4] "Protestant servants and tenants (says Mr. Wakefield) are arrogant, and consider themselves a superior order of men; which, in some degree, arises from their being allowed the use of arms—a privilege denied to the Catholics. This exclusion, as it points out to them their own weakness, draws them, like animals in a storm, closer together."

During the reign of the Penal Code, Mr. O'Connor tells us, the "Roman Catholic gentlemen evaded prosecution by registering their arms in the name of their Protestant servants, whom the law recognized as freemen, though it stamped their masters as slaves. Thus the Catholic gentry contrived means of defence against midnight assassination, and of redress against upstart insolence."—See, in Scully's Penal Laws, a statement of the extent to which this infringement on the Rights of Self-Defence still exists.

10

are sacrificed at every step to the immunities of others, and kept, as game, for a few privileged persons to torment—ask any and all of these, why they are thus persecuted, and when they answer you with that proverb, which sorrow has engraven on their very hearts, "there is no law in Ireland for a Catholic,"—if you *still* think Emancipation unnecessary, go, vote with Mr. Peel—appeal to God and the Constitution with Lord Eldon—talk guard-room politics with the Duke of Wellington—rave of Jesuits with Sir Thomas Lethbridge—write mad pamphlets with Sir Harcourt Lees—drink deep to the Glorious Memory with Sir Abraham Bradley King '— in short, do every thing that is most absurd, frantic, and mischievous—Captain Rock will take you to his bosom as a true and devoted friend, and enrol you along with the illustrious personages just mentioned, as one of the best and most useful consolidators of his power.

CHAPTER XII.

1798—1800.

The Captain's views of his own interest.—The Government acts up to them.—Rebellion of 1798.—The People provoked into it.—The Union. —Secular Odes of Ireland.—Conclusion.

I HAVE already, in a preceding Chapter, acknowledged, that the lucid interval of Lord Fitzwilliam's administration alarmed me. At that moment, could I have introduced myself, as a sort of political Mephistopheles, into the confidence of Mr. Pitt, I would have said to him, "Great minister! this will never do—it is contrary to the whole natural course of rule in Ireland. Here is Lord Fitzwilliam, not only about to deprive of their birth-right that select knot of Protestant gentlemen, who have derived from their ancestors the privilege of mis-governing Ireland, but even forming a plan to introduce, in place of their monopoly, a system of law, moderation, and equal rights. Never was such a thing heard of since the days of Brian Borumhe!

"Still worse—there is, at this moment, a conspiracy organizing; and such a one as a Government with any taste for phlebotomy would rejoice at. It is, as yet, confined to the Protestants and Presbyterians of the North; but the Catholics, if left in their present state of discontent, or, at all events, if goaded according to the old esta-

---

' I have not done justice here to one-half of the "Dii Majores" of Orangeism; and must therefore, to supply the deficiences, refer to a list of "Loyal Public Characters," given in a book called "the Williamite," as the standing Toasts of all Orange Lodges. Mr. Peel, who has naturally a spirit "touch'd to finer purposes," will there see with what luminaries his No-Popery politics constellate him:

blished method, will inevitably join it. Yet, so lost are the examples of history upon Lord Fitzwilliam and Mr. Grattan, that—instead of availing themselves, as they ought, of such a glorious opportunity for confusion—they are actually, while I address you, meditating a measure, which will content the Catholics, disconcert the United Irishmen, squeeze the black drop (as the angel did with Mahomet) out of the heart of the Protestant Ascendancy—and, in short, make eleven twelfths of the people happy and peaceable, to the utter extinction of the tyranny and mischief of the remaining handful!

"This, I repeat it, will never do—shades of Sir William Parsons and Primate Boulton forbid it! You must recall Lord Fitzwilliam —restore the Ascendancy to that power, which it knows so well how to abuse—send us over a Governor, not too wise, who will let Lord Clare and the Beresfords be viceroys over him—give full loose to the loyalty of the Orangemen, those hereditary scourges of the country '—let them again yell in the ears of the Catholics the old Cromwell cry of, ' to Hell or Connaught,' and, lest any fear of the laws should damp their generous ardour, let Indemnity shine out in the distance, as their beacon through desolation and blood— confine not the exercise of tyranny to the Government, but delegate it throughout the whole privileged class; and multiply the scorpions on your whip, till you leave no single part of the victim unreached by them—' do this, and Cato will be Cæsar's friend'—do this, and depend upon it, the results will be such, as even the ' wisdom of our ancestors' would not have blushed to acknowledge.

"In the first place, by your adoption of this system, we shall none of us be disappointed of our rebellion—neither the Faction of the Rocks, whom centuries of defeat have not discouraged, nor the Faction of the Ascendancy, whom centuries of triumph have not

---

' These wishes and plans of the Captain were all realized. "The Orangemen, in 1796," says a Protestant writer, well acquainted with those times, "commenced a persecution of the blackest dye. They would no longer permit a Catholic to exist in the County (Armagh). They posted up on the cabins of those unfortunate victims this pithy notice, ' to Hell or Connaught,' and appointed a limited time, in which the necessary removals of persons and property were to be made. If after the expiration of that period, the notice had not been entirely complied with, the Orangemen assembled, destroyed their furniture, burnt the habitations, and forced the ruined family to fly elsewhere for shelter. In this way upwards of 700 Catholic families in one County were forced to abandon their farms, their dwellings, and their properties, without any process of law, and even without any alleged crime, except their religious belief be one."

Out of this aggression, naturally rose that association of the lower orders, called Defenders; and while these were hanged without mercy wherever they appeared, the Orangemen, on the contrary (says Mr. Grattan), "met with impunity, and success, and triumph. They triumphed over the law—they triumphed over the magistrates, and they triumphed over the people."

satisfied. In the next place, by lashing up the lowest of the populace [1], into a fury as blind as that of the Cyclops in his cave, but
only the more ferocious for being unenlightened, you will throw
the tarnish of bigotry over the banner of Freedom, and bring disgrace for ever upon the cause of the people in Ireland. In the third
place, by the opportunity of abundant blood-letting, which the
popular inflammation you have provoked will furnish, you will be
enabled to cool down the temperament of the country, into a state
tame enough for the reception of a Union [2] — and finally, by that
Act, will deliver up Ireland, bound hand and foot, into the fangs
of Captain ROCK and the Ascendancy, to be their joint prey through
all succeeding times.''

Such was the advice, dictated by the truest spirit of Rockism,
and founded on a familiar acquaintance with the wisdom of other
times, which I would, at that moment, have given worlds to whisper
into the ear of the British minister. But I soon found it unnecessary
—a Mephistopheles was not wanting. Mr. Beresford, on the first
alarm of the intended inroad upon monopoly, had hastened over
to London, and pleaded the cause of the Ascendancy and injustice
with such success, that all idea of disturbing their ancient reign
was abandoned. No sooner had the Minister obtained the enormous
grant of one million seven hundred thousand pounds, which, on
the faith of the promised measures was patiently acquiesced in,
than those measures were withdrawn — Lord Fitzwilliam recalled [3]

---

[1] So little was this intention concealed in 1797, that an English fencible regiment actually issued a sort of manifesto to the Catholics of Ireland, calling them
".infamous and dastardly," and challenging them to stand forth—adding, that "they
did not come into this country to be trifled with."

[2] In a communication from the English Cabinet to Lord Fitzwilliam at the
time, this design was pretty clearly intimated. The postponement (it was there
said) of the intended concessions to the Catholics, "would be not merely an expediency or a thing to be desired for the present; but the means of doing a greater
good to the British empire than it had been capable of receiving since the Revolution, or at least since the Union." Lord Fitzwilliam, too, in his answer, appears
to have fully understood the stimulating system that was about to be pursued, as
he refused " to be the person to raise a flame, which nothing but the force of arms
could keep down."—Letters to Lord Carlisle.

Compare these circumstances with the delay of the promised Graces under
Charles, and observe how closely the parallel is preserved throughout. It was said
of Ovid " Non ignoravit vitia sua, sed amavit," and a similar love for their own
iniquities is observable through every page of the history of our rulers.

[3] Mr. Duquerry, who had opposed Lord Fitzwilliam's administration on the
subject of the war, yet strongly felt and deprecated the dangerous consequences
of his recall; and severely animadverted upon the conduct of Mr. Pitt, who,
" not satisfied," he said, " with having involved the empire in a disastrous war,
intended to complete the mischief by risking the internal peace of Ireland—

— and the system which I had set my heart upon instantly put into practice, with a vigour of execution [1] which surpassed my most sanguine expectations:.

I have already had occasion, in remarking upon some extracts from a Journal, kept by one of my ancestors in the great Rebellion of 1641. to compare briefly the events of that period with those of 1798, and to show the family resemblance that existed between the two Rebellions. Both born in the perfidy of the government, and both nurtured into strength by its cruelties, they each ran the same career of blood, and each, in expiring, left its unburied corpse, to poison the two parties that still sullenly contended over it.

As the policy of our rulers was so like at both periods, so the persons, selected to carry it into effect, were equally well suited to the mission intrusted to them; and the names of Coote, St. Leger, Tichborne, etc. in 1641, may find *pendants* among our military heroes of 1798—too recent, perhaps, to be hung up in the Gallery of History, but quite as worthy of the cause in which their zeal was signalized.

There was, however, in the choice of instruments at this latter period, one egregious mistake committed by the Government. The bravery, good sense, and humanity of Sir Ralph Abercromby were all misplaced in that wretched warfare, where the soldier was sent to *make*, not to *meet* enemies, and the lash and the picket went before, to cater for the bayonet [2]. Accordingly, during the short time of this gallant soldier's command, his moderation and

---

making the friends of the country the dupes of his fraud and artifice, in order to swindle the nation out of 1,700,000*l.* to support the war, *on the faith of measures which he intended should be refused.*"

[1] The scene that followed is thus forcibly and truly described in a publication of that time. "Coercion and terror became the order of the day. The astonished citizen beheld laws of death daily issuing from that seat of legislation; where a few weeks before, he had fondly hoped to see the peace-offering of a united people received with gratitude by an honoured government. The lash, the prison and the rope were rapid, yet too slow in their devastation; foreign troops poured in from every quarter, and military superseded civil law. But law of any kind, even military law, was thought too merciful;" etc. etc.

[2] The following is by no means an overcharged statement of some of the means by which the rebellion was ripened. "If industrious peasants are to be, at the beck of any spy, informer, or perjured approver, dragged from their habitations, and the embraces of their wives and children, parents or relatives, at the dead hour of the night, and hanged and shot at their own thresholds, without the semblance of trial, or time to implore the mercy of heaven in their last moments: —if the cottage of the husbandman is, upon similar grounds, to be consigned to conflagration, and its miserable inhabitants shot or stabbed for endeavouring to escape from the flames: —if the peaceable Catholics of a whole district, nay, of whole counties, are to be banished from their country, their little property, and means of livelihood, by the edict of a paid, protected, and nefarious banditti

good feeling stood considerably in the way of his employers. When sent into Kildare to quell an insurrection, he found all quiet—and understood his orders so little as to leave all quiet as he found it. The army, too, which, before he took the command, was cheered along in its course of devastation both by Church and State, and could hardly burn, shoot, stab and violate fast enough for its patrons and admirers, was by him branded with a public and indignant rebuke for its licentiousness, and pronounced to be "in a state which made it formidable to every one but the enemy."

Such honesty was, of course, out of harmony with the existing system, and Sir Ralph Abercromby found it necessary to resign—well repaid for the loss by his own heart's approval ever after, and by that blessing which consecrates the memory of the few, who have, in Ireland, stood between the oppressor and the oppressed.

With respect to the atrocities committed by some members of my Family, during the paroxysm of that re-action which the measures of the Government had provoked, it is far from my intention to enter into any defence of them. I will merely say, that they who, after having read the preceding pages, can still wonder at such events as even the massacre of Scullabogue, [1] have yet to learn that simple theory of the connexion of effects with their causes, which is the sovereign cure for wonder on all such occasions.

We now come to the consummation—to the harvest reaped from all this blood. Forfeitures were, as we have seen, the price paid by Ireland for her former rebellions—and the forfeiture of her existence as a nation was the mulct imposed upon her for this.

So proud was Mr. Pitt of his achievement of the Union, that he regarded it as a matter of triumph to *begin* the century with it. Alas for the Muse of Ireland! *Her* Secular Odes have thus always been dirges of slavery and sorrow. The Seventeenth Century opened with the perfidy of James, who first flattered the hopes of the Catholics, and then persecuted and plundered them afterwards—the birth of the Eighteenth was signalized by the violation of the Article of Li-

called Orangemen, and their houses burned about their ears for non-compliance," etc.

When some of these outrages were stated by Lord Moira in the English House of Lords, a Noble Minister, in denying the truth of the statement, said that "the people would resist and resent, if it was so." The people took the hint.

[1] Even this, too, may be traced to the panic which the severities of the Government had diffused. "Some run-away rebels," says Mr. Gordon, "declaring that the royal army in Ross were shooting all the prisoners, and butchering the Catholics who had fallen into their hands, feigned an order from Harvey (the rebel leader) for the execution of those persons at Scullabogue. This order, which Harvey, himself a Protestant and a man of humanity, was utterly incapable of giving, Murphy is said to have resisted—but his resistance was in vain."

merick—and the Union, a measure rising out of corruption and blood, and clothed in promises put on only to betray, was the phantom by which the dawn of the Nineteenth was welcomed.

The proclamation of the Herald in the Secular Games of the ancients, was—"Come ye unto sports which no mortal hath ever seen nor ever shall see." But to us the revolution of ages brings no such novelty, and the words of our Herald, Time, should be—"Come ye unto the misery and the slavery which your fathers endured before you, and which it is the will and the wisdom of the Legislature that your children should suffer after you!"

I clearly foresaw the advantages that a Union would bring to my Family; nor was I singular in this view of the consequences of that measure. Mr. Saurin (the late Attorney General) in a Speech delivered on the 21st of February, 1800, in the Irish House of Commons, thus strongly foretold the great accession of strength which would ensue from a Union to the ROCK interest: "Is it by such a project and such a measure that we believe Ireland can be tranquillized, or her distractions and dissensions removed? *No, Sir;—is it not, on the contrary, adding to and augmenting her divisions and distractions, by a new sort of division and distraction, which will last, in all human probability, for another century, with rancour and fury?*" Mr. Foster, too, (now Lord Oriel,) was equally clear-sighted in prophesying the consequences that have since resulted from the measure—declaring that a Union would have no other effect than that of turning Ireland into "*a discontented province.*"

Aware, however, as I was of all this—and fondly as my fancy already revelled in the clear field of combat, which the removal of the Parliament would leave to me and the Ascendancy, yet could I not help shuddering, from a sort of Irish instinct, at the act of national degradation that was now about to be exhibited to the world.

When I saw the boon of Emancipation held temptingly to the lips of the Catholic, like that dear-bought draught at Cleopatra's banquet, with the pearl of his country's Independence dissolved within it—scarcely could I help joining the few voices that exclaimed, "What! will you surrender your country for a shadow? Will you trust to those, who have deceived you so often, and cease to be Irishmen, in the vain hope of becoming freemen?

"The bargain of our parliamentary Judases is, at least, intelligible and tangible, and the 'thirty pieces of silver' on the palm acquits them of being romantic in their treason. But what have *you* in exchange for this surrender of national existence? The verbal pledge of a minister—the fairy money of Hope, which seems gold to the eye, but will turn into dust in the hand!

" Be assured that a Union will put Emancipation farther off than ever. 'Once merged in the Empire (say your deceivers), your numbers will be no longer formidable, and you may with safety be admitted into the Constitution[1].' Once merged in the Empire (say I), your numbers will, indeed, cease to be formidable—but, *therefore*, you will no longer be of importance, and, *therefore*, you will not be emancipated. It was only from the fears and interests of a resident Legislature, acted upon at every point by the pressure of your increasing population, that the few immunities you now enjoy could ever have been extorted—and had the Union been achieved, as was contemplated, in 1785, it would have been then, as it will be now, an *estoppel* to your enfranchisement for ever!"

In my younger and romantic days, I might, perhaps, have been generous enough, to waste (for it would have been no more) a few such warnings on the Catholics. But—even had I been so singularly disinterested as to sacrifice my own advantage to that of my country —the current had then set too strongly in my favour to be resisted, and the projects of the Government for my aggrandizement would, as usual, have succeeded in spite of me.

The shame of Corruption, like the blessing of Mercy, falls alike on "him who gives, and him who takes,"—and at the period of the Union this reciprocity of disgrace was perfect. The Protestant Parliament was purchased with solid bribes—the Catholic people were won over with deceitful promises, and the Minister, glorying in his triumph over both—

> " Gave Liberty the last, the fatal shock,
> Slipp'd the slave's collar on, and snapp'd the lock."

HERE ends the Manuscript of the Captain. He had prepared, as he told me, materials for the continuation of his Narrative, from the Union down to the present day; but the great press of political business which that measure brought upon him, left him but little leisure for the indulgence of literary pursuits.

As the Law and the Captain are always correlative in their movements, the state of the *one* during any given period will always enable us to judge of the activity of the *other*. It has been said,

[1] Mr. Grattan thus states this argument of the Minister:—"For this hope he exhibits no other ground than the physical inanity of the Catholic body, accomplished by a Union, which. as it destroys the relative importance of Ireland, so it destroys the relative proportion of its Catholic inhabitants, and thus they become admissible, because they cease to be anything." Hence, according to him, their brilliant expectation. " You were," says he, " before the Union as four to one— you will be by the Union as one to four."

that " you may trace Ireland through the Statute-book of England,
as a wounded man in a crowd is tracked by his blood"—and the
footsteps of the Captain are traceable, in like manner, through the
laws that have prevailed during the last four-and-twenty years. For
instance :—

The Insurrection Act, in force from 1800 to 1802.
Martial Law, in force from 1803 to 1805.
The Insurrection Act, in force from 1807 to 1810.
Ditto, from 1814 to 1818.
Ditto, from 1822 to 1824. '

Well knowing how much the time of the Captain must be taken
up, by the increased demands upon his activity which such a state
of the law implies, I forbore to press him for the remainder of his
Manuscript; choosing rather—though anxious to give the public
the full advantage of his lucubrations—to wait till some interval of
retirement from business, should enable him, like Napoleon at
St. Helena, to put a finishing hand to his Memoirs.

Such an opportunity is now but too likely to be afforded, by an
event that occurred about two months since.

One evening, during the mild weather which prevailed at that
time, the Captain, who is rather of a romantic disposition, was, it
seems, indulging himself with a walk by moonlight on the banks
of the river Suir—meditating, no doubt, on the events of his long
life, and sighing after that peace which he *might* have enjoyed, had
the measures of the Government not forced him into such riotous
distinction. From this reverie he was awakened by the tramp of
horses, and saw rapidly advancing towards him a party of that
gendarmerie, to whom, at present, is confided the task of civilising
Ireland.

Supposing that they knew him, and that his final hour was come,
he, with his usual promptitude, prepared for resistance—having

' "In addition to these Acts (says Sir Henry Parnell, in the excellent Speech
from which this statement is taken), others of a similar unconstitutional kind
have been passed within the same period. The Habeas Corpus Act was suspended
from 1797 to 1802; again from 1803 to 1806; and again in 1822. The Arms Act,
allowing domiciliary visits, and prohibiting the use of arms, was in force from
1796 to 1801, and has been in force from 1807 to the present time, and now
forms part of the standing law of the country. The Peace Preservation Act, by
which a regular gendarmerie was appointed, has been in force from 1814 to the
present time."

"Taking together," he adds, "the periods of disturbances, as before mentioned, with the periods for which the Martial Law and Insurrection Acts have
been in force, we shall find that out of a period of the last thirty-one years, no
less than twenty-six have been years of insurrection or disturbance."—*Speech,
delivered Tuesday, June* 24, 1823.

long resolved (as he himself expresses it), "on the principle of the Sibyl, to sell the last leaf dearly." Perceiving, however, that they were not aware of the rank of their antagonist, and holding it to be the part of a wise man to reserve himself for future chances, he quietly submitted, and was conducted to the gaol of Tipperary.

A Sessions under the Insurrection Act being always ready in that town, he was tried the following day, and the crimes with which he was charged, were—Firstly, being out in the open air by moonlight, and Secondly, not being able to give an account of himself. Of the unfairness of the latter charge, the Public, after having read the preceding pages, can sufficiently judge, though the case, it must be owned, is somewhat different, when the auto-biographer stands before a magistrate under the Insurrection Act.

It appears that there were, in the Court and the Town, at the time, a large assemblage of ROCKITES—any one of whom could have identified our hero, so as to give the going Judges the triumph of, at last, hanging the Real CAPTAIN ROCK. But the only virtue, which the Irish Government has been the means of producing in the people, is fidelity to each other in their Conspiracies against it. Accordingly, the Captain—though shrewdly suspected of being the Captain—was, luckily for himself, not known to be such; and being found guilty only of the transportable offence, namely, that of being out by moonlight, is at this moment on his way to those distant shores, where so many lads "who love the moon" have preceded him.

As every thing that relates to such great men is, in these times, a matter of public interest, I am happy to have it in my power, from the report of an eye-witness, to state that the Captain was dressed, on the morning of his embarkation, in an old green coat —supposed to be the same, but without the yellow facings, which was made up for Napper Tandy, as an officer of the Irish National Guard—a pair of breeches, the colour of which the reporter unluckily could not ascertain, and stockings, of the staple manufacture of Mr. Dick Martin's Kingdom of Connemara.

He was observed to smile as he mounted the side of the vessel, and trod the deck, I am assured, with a very firm step. The state of his mind, however, may best be judged, by the following Extract of a Letter which I received from him, about a week before he sailed.

"*Cove Harbour*, 1824.

* * * * * * * * * * * * *
* * * * * * * * * * * * *

"It is amusing enough that this should be my fate, after all;

though to you, I know, it will afford matter of serious thought. When, after turning over the first pages of the history of our connexion with England, you reflect that now—at the end of six hundred years—an Irishman may be transported, under English laws, for being out of his house (having none, perhaps), after sunset, it will confirm you, I think, still more in the idea impressed upon you while here—that, much as we, of the Rock race, require instruction, our rulers, of every race, require it still more.

"For myself, I am grown old in the service—repose has, at length, become welcome, if not essential, to me; and, when all that a man wishes is, to be able to say, ' inveni Portum ', Port Jackson, perhaps, will do as well as any other.

"For the safety of the Rock Dominion in Ireland, to which my son, now invested with the title of Captain, succeeds, I see but little in the measures or projects of our present rulers to alarm me. On the contrary, it appears to me, that I leave every thing most comfortably calculated, to render the reign of my son as tempestuous and troublesome as my own.

"A Lord Lieutenant, whose enlightened and liberal intentions alarm and offend the stronger party; while his limited powers and embarrassed position incapacitate him from gaining the confidence of the weaker—a Secretary, worthy of the good old Anti-popery times, and to whose spirit I would ensure a safe passage over Mahomet's bridge into Paradise, if *narrowness* (as it is probable) be a qualification for the performance of that hair-breadth promenade —the Orange Ascendancy flourishing under the very eyes of the Government, and imitating that Oligarchy mentioned by Aristotle, whose oath was, 'We will do the multitude all the evil in our power'—the Established Clergy still further enriched, and threatening to ' push ' the Landed Gentry ' from their stools'—more than a million spent annually upon soldiers ', to keep down the Catholics, and only a few thousands per annum given to educate them—with such actual results of the policy of our present rulers, and with Mr. Peel, Lord Eldon, and the duke of Wellington in the Cabinet, to answer for the complexion of their future measures, I may safely, I think, reckon upon the continuance of the Rock Dynasty, through

' "This enormous sum (1,334,967*l.* 6*s.* 10½*d.*) forms only a part of the contributions of Great Britain, to uphold that system of mis-government, to which all the miseries of Ireland, and the destitute condition of her population should be traced. The other expenses, direct and indirect, would certainly increase the annual charge (1823) to two millions sterling, at least. Let the British Senator, therefore, reflect that the condition of Ireland is no longer an Irish question alone, but one most materially affecting the financial concerns of Great Britain." —*Practical Hints and Suggestions, etc. etc.*

many a long year of distraction and tumult; and may lay my head upon my pillow at Botany Bay, with the full assurance that all at home is going on as prosperously as ever.

"A word or two more, my dear Sir, and I have done. As I know you are one of those who have sincerely set their hearts upon the conversion of the Irish Roman Catholics to Protestantism, I will—to show you how little I am under the Influence of bigotry—mention the only mode that has ever occurred to *me*, as affording even a chance of attaining that object. Let an Act be passed, transferring to the Roman Catholic Clergy all the Tithes that are at present paid to the Protestant Establishment; and, if *that* does not alienate the whole body of Roman Catholics from their Pastors, the case is desperate, and you must be content to let Ireland remain Popish.

"Yours, my dear Sir, very truly,

"DECIMUS ROCK,
"*Late Captain of all Ireland.*"

"P. S. I trust to your discretion and honour for not mentioning the circumstances of my fate till you know that I am fairly out of the hands of the Joshuaites—having hanged so many dozens of *wrong* CAPTAIN ROCKS they might possibly now take it into their heads to hang the *right* one."

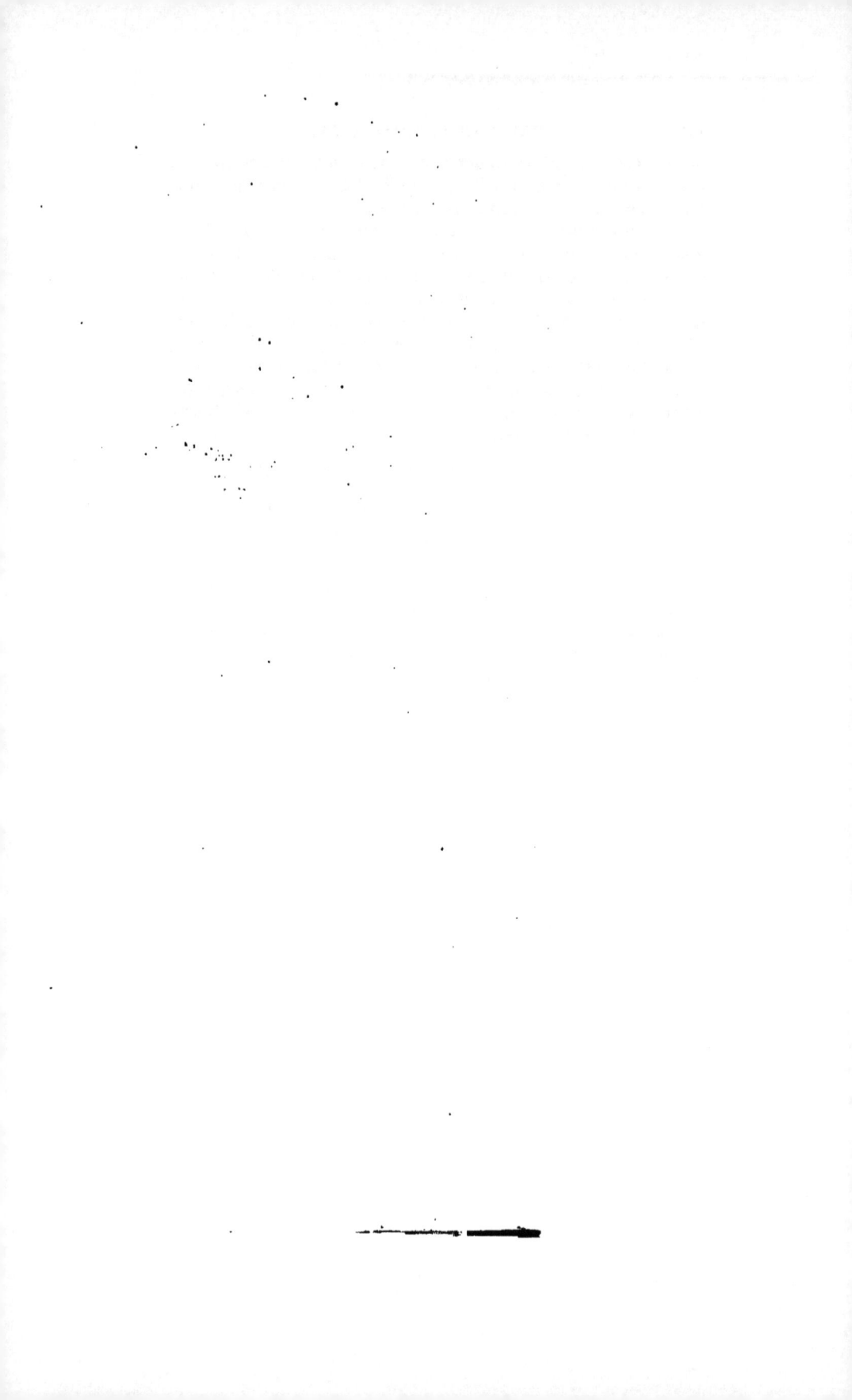

Lightning Source UK Ltd.
Milton Keynes UK
UKHW020633060223
416537UK00012B/2707